Faith in Christ

Faith in Christ

The Journey Out of Loneliness

Joseph Sgro

iUniverse, Inc.
New York Lincoln Shanghai

Faith in Christ
The Journey Out of Loneliness

Copyright © 2007 by Joseph R. Sgro

All rights reserved. No part of this book may be used or reproduced by any means, graphic, electronic, or mechanical, including photocopying, recording, taping or by any information storage retrieval system without the written permission of the publisher except in the case of brief quotations embodied in critical articles and reviews.

iUniverse books may be ordered through booksellers or by contacting:

iUniverse
2021 Pine Lake Road, Suite 100
Lincoln, NE 68512
www.iuniverse.com
1-800-Authors (1-800-288-4677)

The views expressed in this work are solely those of the author and do not necessarily reflect the views of the publisher, and the publisher hereby disclaims any responsibility for them.

The Bible quotations in these pages are from The King James Version.

ISBN: 978-0-595-42836-6 (pbk)
ISBN: 978-0-595-87175-9 (ebk)

Printed in the United States of America

Contents

Acknowledgments vii
Introduction xi
    I Am There xiv
Chapter One A Lost Sheep 1
    I'll Walk With You 5
Chapter Two Years of Wandering 8
    I'll Live Again 10
Chapter Three Setting the Course 12
    Doorway to Heaven 16
Chapter Four Unfamiliar Waters 18
    Follow Me 21
Chapter Five The Message of Jesus 24
    My Friend, My God 27
Chapter Six How Do I Connect To Jesus? 30
    Knights of Christ 32
Chapter Seven Is Church Necessary to Connect to Jesus? ... 35
    The Gates of Heaven 37
Chapter Eight Jesus Is Everywhere 40
    Where Is Jesus? 42

Chapter Nine A Life of Death 45
   Sounds of Heaven..47
Chapter Ten The Promise 50
   Your Promise...53
Chapter Eleven The Death of a King... 56
   Upon My Cross...59
Chapter Twelve An Empty Presence... 63
   A Tree of Torn Hearts 66
Chapter Thirteen A Torn Heart 68
   Falling From Faith...71
Chapter Fourteen A Deep Rooted Love... 74
   My Love for You 76
Chapter Fifteen Is Love Perfection? 78
   Perfection or Love?..81
Chapter Sixteen Tears of Hope... 83
   Rain of Tears...85
Chapter Seventeen Man vs. God 88
An Invitation 91
About the Author 93

Acknowledgments

I WANT TO TAKE A FEW MOMENTS to thank not only all those who have been so kind to me through the years, but also to thank those who are helping me along the path of learning of our Lord Jesus.

First of all, I thank my parents Bertha and Joseph, two of the most loving people God ever put on this earth. To these two I owe everything. Their courage in giving birth to children and accepting the challenge to raise those children is enough to inspire anyone. It was their love and devotion, not only to their children but also to each other, that has built the solid foundation that I now stand upon. That foundation has carried me through many storms and will continue to do so for the rest of my life. Even though they are gone from me now, I know that they still reside here with me, for I feel them. I know that one day when I leave this earth for the trip to the Kingdom of God, there at the gates of heaven, my loving parents will be waiting for me. I know this to be true, for that is the promise of our Lord Jesus Christ.

The next person I want to thank is my brother Vito. Although we never got along very well during our younger years, after my parents passed on, he and I became closer. I'll always remember the Mets game he took me to. He may have forgotten, but I never will.

Vito, we have fought a lot through the years, but you're still my blood, and I'm proud to say you're my brother. I also hope that you know that I truly think you have come a long way and are doing a fine job of taking care of your family. You and I must never let go of Jesus.

Now for my loving wife Margie—there are no words that can describe how I feel for her. Even though we tease each other, sometimes a bit too much, I love her with all my heart. I dread those days that we are apart, because without her, I truly am nothing. Margie gives me life; she *is* my life. She is a hard working woman who is down-to-earth and very considerate. Her heart is made of gold, and her big, brown eyes make me melt.

Babe, you're the one I live for. Each and every day is special to me because it gives me a chance to spend it with you. May God bless us with many more days to enjoy together.

To my daughter Ashley, both your mom and I are very proud of you. I am so happy that we have a relationship deeper than just that of a father and daughter. We're friends, and I love to just have fun with you. You have helped me more than you could ever imagine. Just know that I'll always be there to help you whatever the situation may be, and remember that you are a very special young lady and very talented. Keep up the writing, because one day you'll realize your dreams.

To Rob, the pastor at our church, what a great guy and fellow pizza-lover. It is his true love of Christ that has helped me along the pathway that I now travel. His wonderful gift of sharing the Gospel has touched my heart.

I must not forget my Bible study crew—Tom, Don, Hillary, and Scott. These guys are truly "The Wild Bunch"! Thanks for allowing me the opportunity to come together with you to dwell within the word of God.

Now for my readers—I wish to thank you for having the confidence in me necessary to not only purchase this book, but also to read it. I want to thank you for allowing me to come into your life and share my story with you.

My purpose in writing comes from Jesus. I asked him how I could repay him for all his help, and, shortly after that, I began to be inspired to write poems. In speaking with him more, I began to realize that perhaps his answer to me was a gift for writing. With this in mind, I decided to put my story together with my poems, and then get it out to the world in the hope that someone like myself, who was lost and feeling alone, could get hold of the book, and that it would lead that person to Jesus.

Jesus is our Savior and he waits for us. He calls us, but we need to open our hearts to him. Please, I implore you; don't turn away. No matter how bad the situation, no matter how lost you may be, know that he is standing not far away, longing to help. Just open your heart and join us on this journey.

Please pass this book onto someone who you think could use a little help in his or her life. In a world that is broken, let us bond together to reach out and show others just what Jesus can do.

All my love, and
May God bless you,
Joseph R. Sgro

Introduction

As I sit, I ponder just where to start. My goal is to put into words my personal journey, what life has taught me, and how what we sometimes call *the obvious* isn't as easily seen as we think. The main reason I write this book is to share my experiences as well as my thoughts on Jesus; I believe the inspiration for writing has come from our Lord.

I have often wondered how I could repay Jesus for all of his help; I don't think that any one of us ever truly could. Still there are many folks who, like I, have reached a point in life where, although successful, we're still missing something. Perhaps that something is Jesus. I truly hope that this book can reach out to those who feel a void but don't know how to fill it. Perhaps I can help someone open his heart to the love of Jesus and so fill that once empty space.

I truly believe the force that drives us comes from within the heart. Our hearts pump the life-sustaining blood through our veins; however, the heart is more than just a pump, more than just an organ. It contains within it the spark of emotion. It can be hardened, or it can be open and loving. From life's onset at birth, life itself seems to begin hardening the heart. As we grow, friends and family add to the mixture of hardening influences.

As time passes, that once wonderfully soft heart seems to grow hard and cold and, sometimes, even with family and many close and devoted friends, we find that the road we walk is an empty one, that we are still alone, feeling the pains of loneliness. That loneliness takes a toll. It is as devastating as an incurable cancer. Not all the doctors or medicines available to us can help, for physically we are fine—or so it would seem.

I once heard it said that a "true friend" is someone who knows what you want or need just when you want or need it. In years past, I would say, "I can't truly think of anyone who fits that description." Now I say, "I have found someone who fits that description perfectly."

In all my years of searching for a true friend, someone to depend on, to talk to, to fall back on, to know would always be there for me, someone who would truly care about me without concern for themselves, I finally began to realize that that friend has always been with me. That friend has been by my side through all my successes and failures. Meeting him had nothing to do with opening my eyes or mind, but opening my heart and simply saying, "Hello, Jesus. May I now walk beside you and call you my friend?" With a warm feeling overcoming me, the answer was simple, "You have only to open your heart to me, and I will take hold and never let go."

Religion is a difficult subject, and each of us responds to it in different ways. There are folks who feel very strongly that you cannot connect with Jesus unless you become a devout believer, one who lives and breathes the gospel. Their belief is that one must give over all of themselves in order to be saved. Going to church on Sunday becomes a must, and if missed, you will fall from grace.

Now, please let me stop here and say that I'm not in any way poking fun at these folks. In my view—and please remember that this is my opinion—Jesus most definitely wants us to believe in him; this is a prime reason that he came to Earth to begin with. Walking among us was necessary in order to bring the word of God to us on a personal level. Also, his being here in the flesh and performing miracles allowed us to, in a sense, see God and his love for us.

Now, God elected to create a new covenant to better reach his children. This new covenant, I feel, was based on love, for that is what

Jesus showed and taught. Love can still be seen through the Old Testament, although possibly hidden from the untrained eye. It took Jesus to explain and show us that God has an unending love for us.

It is this new covenant—or *New Testament*—that has captured my attention. I find it truly interesting that in the book of Hebrews, God said, and I'm quoting from chapter 10, *"This is the covenant that I will make with them after those days, saith the Lord, I will put my laws into their hearts, and in their minds I will write them; And their sins and iniquities I will remember no more."*

I view this as God saying how much he loves us, and helping us understand his love better. He is going to impress his laws, love, words, and commandments within us. So all we need to know or understand is within us from the start.

The key is to tap into it.

I am just now finding out how much I am capable of. All I need to do is ask for help, and it is given. I am learning there is nothing to fear, for if I do become afraid, all I have to do is remember that Jesus is beside me. If I am unsure of how to proceed, I trust that Jesus will show me the way.

I have promised to be self-sustaining and to learn so as not to be a burden. I have told Jesus that I want him as my friend and not my caretaker. I have begun to read his teachings, and I am beginning to understand that the teachings have always been within me, for it is I who allow my heart to be hardened and thus soil myself. As do others. We do this for many reasons that I will not touch upon, for saying it is so is enough.

My journey is just beginning, and I still am not sure how to approach my Creator. I need to learn more of him, but he already knows this, for he gave us Christ—the one and only Christ who will always love us and guide us through our journey of life. Even greater then this, we will find ourselves in awe as we walk the path through the heavens with Jesus by our side.

* * * *

"I AM THERE" IS A POEM that hits close to home for me. I never truly believed in God or ever wanted to go to church, and now, well, here I am, on the journey of a lifetime. I wrote these verses because those years I lost through hard-heartedness don't really matter. Why? Because Jesus has always been there for me. When I was born, he loved me; when I rebelled, he loved me; when I came to him broken, he not only loved me but spoke to my heart while holding me in his loving arms. And when he whispers into my ear, "My child, it's time to come home," I will go to him, and he will love me.

So truly, there are no wasted years. Jesus has always been there waiting, watching, guiding, and—most important of all—loving. How could anyone expect anything else, knowing that he died for us upon a cross? My Lord was tortured, disgraced, abandoned, and nailed to a wooden cross to die for me, and he did it willingly.

Who am I to deserve that kind of love? Well, I must be somebody special to him, and that makes sense, for I would do the same for my daughter, for she is my child and is a part of me. I would not question the call to lay down my life for her any more than Jesus questioned his call to lay down his life for me. You see, I am a part of him just as you are; he lives inside of us all, he is so real, and I am at a loss as to why it is that we can miss his presence. Well, that's the background for what inspired me to write "I Am There"

I AM THERE

When you enter into this world,
And you're fragile and you're weak,

There is hope and there is love.
You need not call; you need not seek.

I am there.

When the sun shines so bright,
And your eyes are full of wonder,
When the clouds fill the sky,
And there's rain, and there's thunder.

I am there.

I am there when you need me.
I am there when you call.
I will always love you.
I will catch you when you fall.
And surely you will know, I am there.

Life is hard; the road is narrow.
When you question, when you doubt,
When you turn and walk away,
There is no walking out.

I am there.

When you're lost and afraid,
When you're lonely and confused,
When the world has turned its back,
And you're beaten and abused.

I am there.

I am there when you need me.
I am there when you call.
I will always love you.

I will catch you when you fall,
And surely you will know, I am there.

When your journey leads you back
And your life has come apart,
I'll take you in my loving arms,
For you never left my heart.

I am there.

When the final journey starts,
And you walk through the unknown,
You needn't call my name,
As you never walk alone.
For I am always with you.
Always … until you're home.

I am there when you need me.
I am there when you call.
I will always love you.
I will catch you when you fall,
And surely you will know, I am there.

Chapter One
A Lost Sheep

GROWING UP, I HAD A STABLE LIFE. My parents never experienced any marital problems; there was no substance or physical abuse. Although I was introverted and didn't have many friends, honestly, I must say that I had a happy childhood. My only brother, Vito, was eight years older than I, so we always had different friends, and for the most part, different lives.

Family wise, well, our extended family wasn't very close; there was always some type of friction in the works. I guess that's the way it is with most families, the difference being that some can overlook the friction and still get together. Ours seemed to let the grudges deepen, and we all grew apart. I adapted by just going with the situation, and through it all, grew closer to my mom and dad.

Being alone most of the time allowed me to develop the ability to think on my own and gave me a stability on which I have drawn many times in my life. So there were no family get-togethers to help me come out of my shell, but that did strengthen me for the future. As I moved through life, I found that I wasn't the only one; many folks have had to deal with the same kind of situation.

Though in many ways, I was alone throughout my early life, I never really *felt* alone. I had some friends and always had my parents close by for support and companionship. Children don't seem to dwell on loneliness, but seem capable of entertaining themselves somehow. As I moved into adulthood I began to feel the need to share my life with someone. Like most young developing adults, I didn't want to go through life alone, so, just as most of us do, I began to search for that soul mate. All the while, I was also trying to establish myself with a career.

Oh, how I could write a book on that exploration—searching for a soul mate! It will be enough to say that this was quite an adventure and *not* the most enjoyable time of my life. I never seemed to make the right connection.

Now, at that point in time, I was not connecting with our Lord Jesus. I had set my mind on not believing in him. Because I didn't *see* him, there was no proof that he existed. Being asked to just believe made no sense to me, and I wasn't buying it.

So I walked many avenues in searching for someone to share my life. Each encounter led to failure, so I almost gave up and began to face the reality that I might have to go through life alone. This was not a happy thought, but with so many failed attempts behind me, I wasn't sure just how to proceed any further. But for some reason—and I can't put my finger on just what that reason was—I began to search for a pen pal. Yes, I know, it sounds so cheap, but that was the direction I moved.

Perhaps I was thinking that a culture change might offer a better match opportunity. But whatever made me think that I could find what I was looking for in a mate by writing letters to someone a world away when I couldn't find someone next door, I can't imagine! No matter, the search was on, and boy, did I find the pot of gold.

Now if I remember correctly, the advertisement said that this organization, *Jewels of the Orient*, offered a brochure with a list of people who were searching for pen pals. This sounded quite interesting, and my curiosity was aroused. So I decided to write in and explore this possibility. Within a short time, I had received a brochure that was chock-full of young ladies from the Orient who were actively looking to find a pen pal.

I wasn't sure that this was a good move, but I gave it some thought. I felt that most of the women I was meeting here in this country were more interested in the material things that I could give them than in a loving relationship. So I decided to give it a try.

As I looked over the brochure, one young lady stood out—in fact, she really caught my eye. Margie was beautiful, and I was attracted to her, so I sat down and wrote to her. My letters to Margie were quite long, and I really put my heart and soul into my words. To my amazement, after my first letter to her, I actually received a letter back. Again, here I thought I was doing all this on my own.

Through our writings, I saw Margie as a very down to earth person who was really looking to share her life with someone and was not too interested in the material things of life. It is true that she lived in a poor country and that coming to America would promise her a better life, but somehow I knew that wasn't her motivation.

Now—some twenty-one years later—I've begun to think that though I didn't believe in Jesus, perhaps Jesus believed in me. You see, I believe now that he was looking at me and feeling my loneliness, feeling my pain. My Lord didn't try to beat me into submission so that I would believe in him. Rather, he gently took me in his arms and helped me find what I needed.

Now at the same time, Margie, my lovely wife-to-be who was living in the Philippines, was experiencing the same pangs of loneliness and having the same difficulty in meeting someone. She wanted to make a better life and prayed for Jesus's help.

Now think of it—two people a world apart, a perfect match, never to meet or perhaps destined to meet. But Margie was very much in touch with Jesus and prayed to him often.

I was just the opposite, closed-minded and cold-hearted, yet he still brought us together. He knew what needed to be done, and he did it. What touches my heart is that Jesus, knowing that I didn't believe in him at that time, still gave of himself to help me, just as he did when he walked to his cross for all mankind.

When I met Margie for the first time, I truly did fall in love with her. As time passed, I knew that she was the one I was searching for, and I asked for her hand in marriage. With two separate trips to the Philippines, I finally was able to bring my lovely wife here to start our life together.

Both Margie and I have found that there is no magic in being married; it's hard work to keep it all going. There are many rough roads to be traveled, and two need to become as one. Easily said, but hard to do. The two of us have rolled up our sleeves and learned to put our differences behind us and make our life together work. There's plenty of give and take, but through it all we find that our love for each other has grown many times from what it was.

Love may be given, but it also has to be earned and cherished in order to grow and blossom. My wife has taught me so much about life, as well as about myself. She has a heart of gold, but more than that, she shines like a diamond. I have often looked back over our married years, and never once have I thought of trading one minute of our time together, no, not for all the riches of the world. You see, I've realized that material riches can never be as precious as the richness of true love.

In looking back over my ups and downs in my search, I see that although I didn't want to believe in a *myth*, as I called him, still that *myth* loved me and believed in me. Jesus believed enough in me to bring Margie and me together.

Perhaps this was his way of gently knocking on my door. I still didn't realize what was happening. I didn't think that there was any divine help here; I just figured that I did it on my own. How stubborn and self-centered we humans are. Just as parents look at their children when they keep repeating the same mistakes over and over, Jesus looks at us and just works harder to reach us. We humans become more and more frustrated with our failures, and we begin to narrow our vision and our minds to try and get it right. In doing so, we lose the perspective of God. Jesus *is* there. He's watching. He's waiting for the proper time to step in and assist. We fail to see this because we want instant gratification. If the problem doesn't get fixed right now, then there is no God. This is so far from the truth, but we blind ourselves to it. Jesus's own words to his disciple Thomas, "because thou hast seen me, thou hast believed: blessed are they that have not seen, and yet have believed."

As you read through the Bible, you'll notice that we're called "the children of God." I find this very interesting. It is a comparison between earthly parent/child relationships and heavenly parent/child relationships. As I see it, there is a strong resemblance. The way we love and teach our children is very similar to the way Jesus cares for and teaches us.

* * * *

JUST KNOWING THAT JESUS walks with me every day was enough to inspire me to write this ...

I'll Walk With You

The sun may be shining,
Though your path may be dim.
You stumble and fall,
Still a hand comes from Him.

You reach out and grab hold,
And He lifts you up.

He carries you in His arms,
For He has drunk from the cup.

His words are burned into your soul.
You have touched the face of God.
The battles will be many,
But the victory will be ours.

"I walk with you,"
Are the words we hear.
No longer are we afraid,
No longer do we fear.
Our Lord and Savior has spoken.
"I walk with you."

I stand tall.
I walk with pride.
I know now that
Jesus is by my side.

Fear and uncertainty no longer
Have a hold on me.
The darkness has now cleared,
And I can now see.

I have the power
To overcome.
Jesus now walks with me.
He calls me friend; He calls me son.

"I walk with you,"
Are the words we hear.
No longer are we afraid,
No longer do we fear.

Our Lord and Savior has spoken,
"I walk with you."

The walk is hard.
The path is long.
The light is shining.
My heart has song.

The love of many
Are united in one.
We are the body,
We are the son.

God has given from His heart
What we needed from the start,
A shining light and word to preach,
Our Lord Jesus to walk and teach.

"I walk with you,"
Are the words we hear.
No longer are we afraid.
No longer do we fear.
Our Lord and Savior has spoken,
"I walk with you."

Chapter Two
Years of Wandering

WITH FINDING MARGIE I thought that things would start to come together, but somehow there was still an emptiness. I didn't think much of it, as I was busy trying to find my place in the working world so I could move ahead. My idea was that by finding that right job and moving up to higher financial grounds, I could buy my happiness and finally leave behind that awkward feeling that something was missing.

Thinking back, that feeling of emptiness was quite a sticking point. No matter what I did, or how hard I tried, I was getting nowhere. I was wandering around aimlessly in the dark. I needed to get on course and start moving in some clear, definite direction.

I had made a decision a few years earlier to attend a technical school, Teterboro School of Aeronautics, and there I had attained my Aircraft and Power Plant licenses. Having the licenses in hand, I could now move into the aviation field as an aircraft technician. I thought this was going to be the avenue to my goal. But when I graduated, the entire aviation industry was in one huge slump, and jobs were nowhere to be found. This put a big kink in my plans.

I realized as the years passed that, although I truly loved aviation, it was a very tough field with many up and down cycles, and that jobs were not now as secure as in the past. Even, if I had gotten a position with one of the major airlines, I would have faced layoffs and/or relocations. Either or both of these would have been devastating. The training I had received in school was broad based and allowed me the opportunity to use those skills in many different fields. This is how I ended up in the aerospace industry.

Even as I was recovering from the aviation disaster, I didn't realize the guidance that I was receiving from the Lord. Now I can look back and see how he was nudging me along a chosen path; the nudging was so gentle that I never noticed it at all. Again, he wasn't trying to overwhelm me, just showing his love for a lost soul. Jesus knew that I had potential, and he wasn't going to lose me; he wasn't going to force himself upon me either. No, he was going to let me come to him on my own. By doing this, I would later realize just how much he was guiding me through those years.

As the years passed, I moved from one company to another, always chasing the dream of making it big. But all the dreams I found were broken. I was caught in the world of company politics. One of the keys to moving up wasn't *what* you knew, but *who* you knew. Moving up meant being a better liar, cheat, and schmoozer. This went against my grain. I couldn't understand how it was that the real world worked this way, but it did. Those who could play the game were able to survive and prosper. Others, who didn't want to play just got by. I was tired of just getting by; I knew there was a way out, a way to grow, to feel that I was doing something of value.

All through this, I didn't have anyone to talk to. Well, that's not totally true. I did have my wife Margie, but she just didn't get it. My parents, who were still alive at this time, knew I was going through a period of finding myself, but they really couldn't help much. They always lent support where they could, and I'll always remember their love and help.

Here's what makes me feel so *unintelligent*—or maybe I should just say *dense* or *thick*—all this time I could have been talking with Jesus.

Not only would I have felt better, but I would also have been able to ask more of his help and guidance. Still, somehow I was closed-minded and stubborn. Oh, how wicked a generation are we, just as he said. Here I had the chance to get the help I needed and to find a friend who would always be there for me when I felt troubled, yet I couldn't see it. I just let myself fall deeper into the darkness and the light at the end of the tunnel seemed to be going out.

* * * *

I'LL LIVE AGAIN

The world is coming to an end, my friends
The world is coming to an end.
I say the world is coming to an end, my friends
The world is coming to an end.

But I'm not scared, and I'll tell you why.
Cause they hung Him on the cross
But He didn't die.
He looked at that devil and spit in His eye.

I'll live again. I'll live again.
By the power of God and the love of the Lord
I'll live again. I'll live again.

People live and people die.
They see the needy and walk right by.
They harden their hearts

And play the game.
They see the cross but forget the name.

Jesus, Jesus was His name.

I'll live again. I'll live again.
By the power of God and the love of the Lord
I'll live again. I'll live again.

Years ago He walked the land
With love in His heart and power in His hand.
He brought the word to one and all.
He lived the life. He lived the call.
He shone like light. He was divine.
He walked to the cross when it was His time.

I'll live again. I'll live again.
By the power of God and the love of the Lord
I'll live again. I'll live again.

The world is coming to an end, my friends.
But don't be scared it's not the end.
Open your hearts and drop to your knees.
Ask the Lord to help you please.
Because on the cross He gave His life.
Gave His life for you and me.

Jesus, Jesus was His name.

I'll live again. I'll live again.
By the power of God and the love of the Lord
I'll live again. I'll live again.

Chapter Three
Setting the Course

AFTER YEARS OF STRUGGLING to find myself, I was left totally lost and frustrated. I was angry with myself for being a failure. The only good thing I had ever done was to marry Margie. And with the birth of Ashley, well, that added more satisfaction to our life. Still, the other things I tried to do just didn't seem to work out for me. That *empty feeling* still lurked in my soul. Perhaps the Lord was still seeking me; I'm not sure. I just know that my life was still not complete. Up until this time, the real world and I did not get along together, and I realized that I was going to have to create my own destiny.

I've always had my own way of thinking, and it never did agree with the way the world worked. My inability to give in to office politics had condemned me to a limited work career. So I began to think of starting my own business. I thought that this might be my way of finding my place in this world. But I also knew how hard it was going to be.

Most businesses fail, and they fail for various reasons. Starting from scratch is very tough. And I didn't know what type of business to start. As I looked over many business opportunity magazines, I realized that there were many companies that promised the world, but in reality were holding out only a fool's pot of gold. I realized that with these, right off the bat, there would be trials and many errors, wasted time, and wasted money. There was going to be a lot of frustration ahead.

I'll run through some of the endeavors I tested and found did not work for me.

First, Margie and I tried the catalog mailing business plan and failed horribly at it. The next business we tried was a vinyl repair program. This had some possibility of success; the repair process worked just fine. With practice, the repaired areas were very hard to notice, and I was pleased with the results. What doomed this business was that the vinyl manufactures began to make the vinyl thinner and thinner, and when it reached a certain thinness, repairs could no longer be made. So once again the business folded.

I had continued to work at my regular job while trying to locate my dream business. It was during this time that Ashley was born. About two years after her birth, Margie and I decided that the city was not where we wanted Ashley to grow-up. We put our heads together and spoke with my mom and dad. At that time, we all—Margie, I, Ashley, and my mom and dad—were living in a two family house. All agreed that it was time to relocate, so we sold the house and moved to our present location in central Jersey.

After having relocated for about a year or so, I started discussing with my father the windshield repair business opportunity. My dad had a keen eye for things like this. He gave it some hard thought and then gave me the thumbs up, so we moved ahead with it. This was our first truly successful business. The repair process worked as advertised and offered a valuable service to customers. We ran that repair business for five or six years and did well with it.

It was during this time that both my parents passed on. Even now it brings tears to my eyes. I miss them so much, and I wish I had spent more quality time with them. If only I had realized back then that money, although important, can never buy back lost time. I try not to think of the past as I look forward to the future and remember the promise of Jesus, that I will again be reunited with my mom and dad.

I noticed that business was falling off, because now the windshield replacement companies were offering the repair services as well. These guys had much larger advertising budgets, and I couldn't keep up with them. Also, to be honest, I missed my dad not being with me. Without him, the business just wasn't the same. So the time had come to close up shop. It had been a very good run, and I'm still proud of that little endeavor.

Ok. Now for the next. Yes, there's still more. The next was our moonwalk rental operation—Margie's and mine. This one was a lot of fun and also a lot of hard work. She and I ran the business together, and Ashley helped out too. It was truly a family business. We ran it for, oh, about seven years before we closed it up. Now the normal question is "Why you would do that?" As I said, it was a very physical business—very hard.

In the east coast region, we could run the operation only during the summer months, and as such, it was never going to be a full time opportunity, not unless we expanded the business to many times its current size. I had thought about it often, but decided that with other small companies opening up and insurance rates rising, plus the fact that Rent-All operations were beginning to offer the moonwalks, it was too big a risk to take.

For two years prior to closing up the moonwalk business, I had given thought to trying to find something that I could work at all year long. Something that would offer a full-time income. I was working as an engineering assistant at the time and was able to do some drafting work. This is what I had wanted to be when in high school, a draftsman. My problem had been that I couldn't draw well. Seems the Lord didn't bless me with an artistic hand! But now, drafting was being done on a computer, so once again the opportunity arose for me to return to my old desire.

I started the drafting business, a small office in my home, and I started to acquire clients. The clientele grew. I saw it was time to go full time with drafting, and it was then that we closed up the moonwalk business.

All has worked out well so far. Again, I look back on all these businesses, and the up's and down's that went with them, and never once through it all did I think of Jesus. When my parents passed on, it was just us against the world—just Margie and I and no one else. How wrong I was! At times like these, I think now that Jesus was not only by my side but was carrying me in his arms.

It was his caring and support that had led me from one thing to another, teaching me how to properly run a business, getting me ready for my real calling, and then fulfilling my true desire, which was to be a draftsmen—a desire from far back in my high school days.

I really feel as if he brought me full circle. There is an old saying that goes like this, "God works in mysterious ways," and it is so true. I'm seeing this in my own life right now.

We need to trust in the Lord; we'll never understand him but we must trust in him. Just as when we ask our parents for advice, and when they give it, we don't fully understand it; but we trust that it's good. Well, it's the same thing, no doubt. Jesus knows what's right. If we're going to believe in him, then we must trust him.

* * * *

I WROTE "DOORWAY TO HEAVEN" thinking of Jesus's teachings of love. It's not so much what you do in life as how you love. He doesn't seek out those who give according to routine; he's looking for those who give of themselves. It has nothing to do with material things or even time; it's all about what comes from the heart.

We think of the heart as a living pump, that it simply moves our blood through the body and sustains our life. But the more I study Jesus, the more I realize that the heart is much more than that. A pump it is, but more than that, it's where our spirit dwells. When emotion moves us, it's the spirit from the heart at work. When we close our minds to Jesus, it's not the brain that closes the door. It's the heart, and that's the key. So when we open the heart to Jesus and believe in him, then we've experienced the miracle of touching him, for his essence dwells within us. All we need to do is "Knock and the door will be opened," hence, "Open up your heart … it's the doorway to heaven."

Doorway to Heaven

As I sit here on the porch
And watch the rain fall,
I listen to the thunder
And hear my heart call.

I read the words of Jesus
And try to understand
The meanings of His message,
His gift to every man

I'm searching for the doorway to heaven.
It's somewhere deep inside us.
The key to this quest
Is in the words of Jesus,
Open up your heart, it's the doorway to heaven

As I walk down the road,
I know not where I go.
All I have with me
Are love, faith and hope.
There's darkness all around me;
I'm searching for the light.
I hear the thunder rumble;
I feel His call of might

I'm searching for the doorway to heaven;
It's somewhere deep inside us.
The key to this quest
Is in the words of Jesus.
Open up your heart, it's the doorway to heaven

So many unanswered questions,
We know not where to turn.
We only know that deep inside,
Our hearts begin to burn.

We know the answer is close,
We think just slightly out of reach.
We must only listen
To the words that Jesus preached.

I'm searching for the doorway to heaven.
It's somewhere deep inside us.
The key to this quest
Is in the words of Jesus.
Open up your heart, it's the doorway to heaven

Chapter Four
Unfamiliar Waters

NOW, FINALLY SETTLING into a full time drafting business, I thought once again that I was on my way. Little did I realize that the inevitable was upon me; I was sailing into unfamiliar waters. Seems like when you least expect it, the calm waters turn into a raging sea, although for me, this storm was something that was going to change my life forever.

Up until the beginning of this chapter, I was giving you a somewhat condensed version of my life. As you can tell it was nothing special, I can truly say that I'm "an average Joe," no pun intended. I was going through my life day to day thinking that I was in complete control, that there were no divine interventions, no angels flying around me—nothing, just me. Did I know of Jesus? Well, yes. I'd heard the story of God's son, the miracles and his hanging on the cross and such, but as I stated once before, I wasn't buying it without proof. So it lingered there, locked up in a closet far back in my mind.

Now comes the fun part. After running the business for about two years from my small office in the basement of our home, I decided that I needed to acquire additional space in order to make things run smoother. So I spoke with Margie, and asked if I could re-work the garage and turn it into an office area. I don't think she was really all with me on it, but as usual, she said to do what I had to do in order to meet my needs. So with her approval, I went to work.

Like many folks, I enjoy a radio for background noise; it makes the day move along and seems to keep one company, especially when you work alone. So I was looking for an easy listening station on my newly purchased radio. Nothing seemed to tune in well, except rock and/or hip-hop music. Not my taste at all, so I kept fiddling with the tuner until I found a strong signal that had a nice sound. So I started listening, and it turned out to be a Christian station—Star 99.1. As soon as I discovered I was listening to a church station, off it went. No way was I going to be preached to all day. I continued to search for something that I could enjoy.

I bounced around from one station to another for a few days, all the while trying to get work done. I settled in on some station that was playing nice music, and I wasn't paying much attention to exactly what I was listening to. It just seemed to fill the void. I didn't realize it, but I had come back to Star 99.1 again.

Then a song come on that actually made me stop working, and I listened to the lyrics. It was Mercy Me's "I Can Only Imagine." It was like I'd been hit with a ton of bricks. Remember that closet way in the back of my mind? Well, someone started knocking on that door!

Again, the Lord works in mysterious ways. After years of ignoring him, he caught my attention with some music and a few words.

Oh how those words made me think!

After hearing that song, I thought to myself, *Let's be honest; when one dies, what could happen?* I truly think the answer is: only one of two things. First—nothing—because there is no God, and the Jesus story was just that, a really good Sunday school story.

The second possibility is that after death, one would come face to face with Jesus. Now, if this were to happen, it might be a little late to start believing in him! There aren't many good excuses to give for ignoring him all your life. I gave this much thought; I put all my heart and soul into it, and decided—at this time in my life—to give Jesus a fair opportunity to show me who he was. (It may have been the other way around, but no matter, the search to connect had begun.)

I continued to listen to the station, trying to absorb all I could so as to make an intelligent decision. I also cracked open an old Bible that my parents had. Funny, it was put away in a closet way up on the top shelf. Another closet—not the one in my office—but the Bible was up top, above everything! I started to read the Old Testament, which was very dry reading. The verbiage was difficult, and I didn't have anyone to talk with who could assist me with understanding. I tried to open up to Margie, but the only help she could give me was, "Read the Bible." This was a tremendous help!

So I continued to try to get through more of the chapters, but just found myself floundering. Some of what I was reading confused me as to the relationship between God and his creation. I began to think that this was going to be a waste of time. So I started to move forward through the other books of the Bible. Still, I didn't find anything that I could latch onto.

And that's when I began to look at The New Testament. And there I found Jesus—sweet Jesus.

Yes, the savior of the world and of my soul. I found him in the pages of The New Testament; I thank God for this! As I read through each book of The New Testament, I found just what I was looking for. The wording made sense to me, and the message was clear; Jesus and God were about love. There was nothing to fear about him; he wasn't a mean God, not at all. He wanted to help us, he wanted to show us a better way, to give us a better life, and most of all, he wanted us to love him.

✻ ✻ ✻ ✻

WHILE DRIVING HOME FROM CHURCH one Sunday, I began to see a vision of Jesus. He was sitting on a large stone teaching the people as he always did. The more Jesus spoke, the larger the crowd grew. He spoke of things foretold long ago, but more than that, he fulfilled those long ago words. His own words carried heart and soul; his personality put forth power and dignity. He spoke with authority; he demonstrated his power by healing the sick and raising the dead.

No matter where he was or what the situation, Jesus always had time to stop and help those in need, for this is why he came to us. The term "love conquers all" fits Jesus to a "T"; he *did* conquer all. When it came his time to leave, I believe he wanted to stay with us a little longer, for he asked if the cup could be taken from him. However, it was his time. His destiny was to go to the cross, and he did it with honor, dignity, and love. Love for all of us. The words that echo in my soul are the words of Jesus saying to us, "Follow Me."

FOLLOW ME

In my travels
Through God's land,
I spread the word,
I made the stand.

I brought the keys
That will set you free.
All you must do
Is follow me.

I am the light.
I am the way.
I shouldered your sins.
I am here to say,
My brothers one and all, follow Me

Fear not the path
You must seek,

For at the end
We shall meet

Heart to heart,
Face to face.
You have a home
In heaven's place,
So follow Me.

I am the light.
I am the way.
I shouldered your sins.
I am here to say,
My brothers one and all, follow Me

The Fathers will
I bring to you.
He is in me
And I in Him too.

The future for all
Is very uncertain
But upon my death,
I became the Curtain.
So follow Me.

I am the light.
I am the way.
I shouldered your sins.
I am here to say,
My brothers one and all, follow Me.

You now have the gift
To be with the Father,

So come one and all,
Sons and daughters.

The way is now clear
I have given for thee.
Now all I ask
Is, follow Me.

I am the light.
I am the way.
I shouldered your sins.
I am here to say,
My brothers one and, all follow Me

Chapter Five
The Message of Jesus

FROM THIS POINT ON, I'm going to put into words what I think Jesus was trying to tell us. I'm a simple person with no formal training in the field of religion, and perhaps this is a good thing. I truly believe that there are many people who are so lost but are afraid to reach out to Jesus because, from previous encounters with others, they were frightened away. Why do I say this? Well, lets think of it; try approaching a divine being, the Creator, this is a very frightening thought.

Just think about it, here is the being who created all there is, and not only this, but he carries on his shoulders the weight of not just the world, but the entire universe. Now take a lost soul, someone who has sinned, been bad, is now broken, and is looking for forgiveness, looking for love, looking for a glimmer of hope in this world of madness. He feels as if he is nothing, not deserving of anything, yet now he must approach God. What goes through his mind—or hers? "God will ignore me." "God will be mad at me." "God will laugh at me." Or perhaps, "He'll send me to hell." The thoughts of the Almighty having to forgive and help someone so insignificant are just unthinkable. So it's better to run away and not face the wrath of God.

If I were facing this situation with all these thoughts of such bad things happening, I, too, would run away as fast as I could, and then I'd crawl under a rock! Now, for those of us who look at Jesus, we see a loving soul. Would I fear Jesus? Never, no matter what I did or what the situation was, I would never be afraid to approach Jesus and ask for help. In my opinion—and please, this *is* my opinion—the Old Testament was replaced with the New Testament. God did this because he was not pleased with the results he was getting from the Old.

Fear is not a good teacher at all, and I think that people of that age felt fear because of the way they were taught and the beliefs that were in place in that century.

Love can reach out across the galaxy and touch a heart faster than fear can whip someone into shape.

God saw this. He knew that we needed to progress through our rebellious stage, and I think he wanted us to know and to have it recorded that he could bring wrath down upon us if needed—just as a parent will paddle a misbehaving child when needed, but his true calling was to love us.

We are slow to learn, and we're not very smart beings. God knew we needed Jesus to explain to us that it was love that God wanted to bring down on Earth, not wrath. We just couldn't understand this concept. We still don't.

All we know is that money and power drive human nature forward. We think they're what we need for existence, that love is just a romantic fairytale for those who live in a world of make-believe. We believe that we're fools to worship a God of love when what we really should do is idolize power and riches, that these are the things that make one significant.

What makes me laugh is that for century's now, people have been chasing the idols of power and riches, and no matter how much of each they manage to acquire, still they fall short of finding their places in life. There is always a lost soul, an emptiness there that not all the power or money can ever fill. Only Jesus can fill that void and bring peace and life to an empty heart.

I think the most difficult thing for us to do is to realize that we must—and I do mean *must*—allow ourselves to let go and give our lives to Jesus. You see, non-believers, as I did, think that this means giving up everything that we treasure to become do-gooders. They think you must go to church on Sunday, pray all the time, help everyone, etcetera.

This is far from the truth. Giving your life to Jesus just means that you're accepting that there is a God—simple as that. It's realizing that we're not alone. A higher being is there, watching, longing to help, to love and to be loved. Perhaps it's the concept of love itself. Some of us think that love is a weakness. When you open your heart to Jesus, you begin to understand that love is *not* a weakness, that it's just the opposite.

This is true power and riches. It's the power of God. It's what drives the universe. It's the essence of the divine. It separates good from evil. It is the deciding factor. He who holds love within his heart, holds all the power of the universe.

I believe that God has put his laws in our hearts and/or in our minds. You see, we already know the Lord; no one needs to teach us about him. He already dwells within us, each of us. We need only open to him and accept him. Believe me, he needs us as much as we need him. We are his children, consequently, we are his life, and his love for us will never end, just as a parent will always love his or her own child. We need not be afraid to say, "I love you, Father." We need not be afraid to say, "Jesus, please help me," or "Please let me into your life," for he's already there waiting, watching, and loving with all his essence. I think his message is simple: God loves you. Embrace that love; it will free you.

* * * *

I can't pick out anything that inspired this writing; it just seemed to happen.

MY FRIEND, MY GOD

Although my life is full of love—
My spouse and child show they care—
There's still an empty space within me
That can only be filled if Jesus is there.

Life is filled with valleys so low
And sometimes peaks of great height,
But when darkness falls upon my soul
Only Jesus can bring the light.

My friend, My God you're always there,
Always loving, always caring.
You see my future and prepare.
You're always helping, always hearing.

Though I try to do my best
I often fail, not knowing why.
I trust you're showing me the way,
And from it all, I'll be lifted high.

The lessons you teach
Are sometimes rough.
To do your will
Can be very tough.

But through it all,
You stay with me,
For thou art my king,
And I love thee.

My friend, My God you're always there,
Always loving, always caring.
You see my future and prepare.
You're always helping, always hearing.
I know you gave your life for me
Upon the cross at Calvary.
I was not on this Earth as yet,
But still, still your mind was set.

Those who were,
And those to come,
You gave your life,
and you are the Son.

When I think of how you suffered,
I can not help but cry.
For all you had to give was love,
Yet still, you chose to die.

The choice was right, it had to be.
Death could not hold you as we did see.
You walked among us once again.
You called us children, you called us friend

My friend, My God, you're always there.
Always loving, always caring
You see my future and prepare.
You're always helping, always hearing.

You are Lord and God of all.
For you Jesus, I hear the call.
I'll walk with you till I can go no more,
And then I'll knock, and you'll open the door,
And when it opens, it's you I'll see,
Waiting there, waiting for me.

And though my life has come to an end,
I'll not cry,
For you're still my friend.

My friend, My God you're always there.
Always loving, always caring.
You see my future and prepare.
You're always helping, always hearing

Chapter Six
How Do I Connect To Jesus?

THIS IS PROBABLY THE MOST IMPORTANT question we can ask. Depending on who you ask, the answer will vary, but I believe the only true way to connect to Jesus is to simply talk to him. Yes, we can connect by going to church or praying to him, and praying is an excellent way to talk with him.

But prayer can take on an elaborate wording that may scare some of us away, so my suggestion is simply this; talk with him just as you would a friend or family member. I think most of us find this the most comfortable way to connect. I always take a few moments in the morning to say a prayer to Jesus and then just chat. I ask that he watch over my family and that he assist those I know who are in need of assistance, be it health or personal problems. Those moments are *our* time, and this is when I just chat with him.

My chatting covers everything from what's going on in my life to dreams I have for the future, problems with work, and my wants and needs as well. This is the best-spent time of the day; I connect to him, and I also get things off my chest. More than this, I'm letting Jesus know what's going on with me. I know that he knows all, but its best that I tell him how I'm feeling about things. Not only does the chatting help me feel better, but at the same time, I'm setting the stage for getting the help I need. Remember, in the Bible, Jesus said, "Ask and it shall be given to you." I find this to be so true. (I just don't ask for the winning lottery numbers!) So many times when faced with a problem and not knowing how to solve it, I've spoken to Jesus about it during a chat session, and a few days later, things have worked out.

If we keep all of our concerns inside, we just destroy ourselves. If you're going to give your life to the Lord, then follow his direction. Talk to him, tell him your concerns and problems; he does listen and will help. It may take a little time, or things may work out a bit differently than you expected, but if you look hard enough, you'll find that he helped you over the rough waters.

Now, I also believe that connecting is a two-way street. Yes, you need to speak with him to develop a good relationship, but you also need to follow his lead. This means helping others when they need it and when you're asked or moved to help. You'll find that at times, you'll see someone in need of help, and for some reason, you just feel its right to lend a hand. Normally you would walk right by, but now you're getting that funny feeling, the yearning to help. This, my friend, is Jesus talking to you, asking you to help someone in need. At first you might want to just walk away, but believe me, he'll talk to your heart, and you'll feel so sorry that you didn't stop to assist that you'll want to kick yourself. So when he speaks to your heart listen to him. Remember, he'll never, never ask you to do anything that exceeds your limits. He'll never put you in an awkward position. Jesus goes above and beyond for us because he loves us, so let's show him that we'll do the same for him.

Once you get used to talking with Jesus and it becomes a normal routine, you'll find yourself talking with him at all times of the day or night. Sometimes a serious conversation, others with a more comical tone, and believe me, Jesus has a sense of humor! How I wish I could have been here when he walked the Earth. I believe that he would have not only been a great teacher, but would have been a lot of fun to be with. His love for life and all living things shine through the Bible passages, and if you read carefully between the lines of text, you'll see that wonderful humor of his.

When Jesus was in the garden praying to the Father, he asked if he could stay with us for a little while longer, yet not as he willed but as the Father willed. Time for Jesus here on Earth was truly short, especially after he started his preaching. In this time, I believe he came to know and love us so much, that although he knew that he must go to the cross to make the impact of his being here, he still wanted to stay a little longer to just be with us. This alone says to me that Jesus saw potential in us to become what were designed to be. He knew that sometimes we go off course, but he has the faith in us to get us back on track. You see, we're like a wilting flower, and with a little loving care, we'll bloom and we'll be awesome.

* * * *

I SOMETIMES FEEL THAT I need to battle the evil that rages inside of me as well as the evil the world throws at me every day. Even though I lose more battles than I win, Jesus picks me up at the end of every day and patches me up for the next day's battles. There are never any harsh words for failing to win, only love to heal.

KNIGHTS OF CHRIST

>We walk with power.
>We march with might.
>We battle the darkness.
>We have the light.

Our armor is strong,
Our bodies are weak.
Our strength comes from Him.
His victory is what we seek.

We are the knights of Christ.
We are the soldiers.
We bring the word.
We battle evil, the
Evil of the world.
We are the knights of Christ.

We march by day.
We watch by night.
We bring love and mercy.
We open eyes and give sight.

To the broken and battered,
To those who can't cope,
We fight for them.
We bring them hope.

We are the knights of Christ.
We are the soldiers.
We bring the word.
We battle evil, the
Evil of the world.
We are the knights of Christ.

The battles rage on,
For they are not few but many.
Souls to be saved,
Our Lord says there are many.

The harvest is rich.
The workers are few.
But we go on.
Fear not, we're coming for you.

We are the knights of Christ.
We are the soldiers.
We bring the word.
We battle evil, the
Evil of the world.
We are the knights of Christ

Chapter Seven
Is Church Necessary to Connect to Jesus?

NO, GOING TO CHURCH IS NOT NECESSARY in order to bond with Jesus. Although, it is a great way to meet others who wish to be close to him and dwell in his home. The church is an important focal point for all things Jesus—in a manner of speaking. There are fellow believers to connect with and various support groups to assist those in need. However, the real connection to Jesus is the opening of your heart, your accepting him, and giving him a chance to help you. You need not be in a church to speak with Jesus; all you need do is just talk with him, anywhere and anytime. Remember he is always with you.

I've found church to be an interesting place to visit. Different churches have different ways of running the services, and experiencing that can be enlightening. However, even Jesus said that you can close the door to your room and pray to the Father, meaning, I feel, that going to a church isn't necessary. As long as your heart is true. You'll find that visiting a church will help you to stay in the spirit of things and assist in keeping the drive going, but don't let it be a stumbling block. If you're thinking about starting to attend a particular church,

I'd suggest you visit once or twice and see if you're comfortable. If you are, then attend every so often. This will allow you to become more knowledgeable about Christ and start making friends who are fellow believers.

In my journey with Christ, I ask his help in understanding, and then I try my best to let him guide me on the path. *I let my heart pull me along.* Now, that's a bit difficult to understand until you are walking with him, but once you are, you'll see what I mean. Bible study groups are nice things to join. I had the pleasure in joining one through a client, and I'm very happy that I accepted the offer. The group is small; only five of us total, and we meet each Tuesday morning for about and hour or so and read a few passages from the Bible.

Our first book was Job; this is a rather long book, so we've been working on it for a while. So I find each week that I'm connecting with other believers, and we're not only growing friendships but also learning the word of God. I was lucky to have had the opportunity to join the group, so I would suggest that this might be a nice way to ease into a deeper understanding of the Bible and to gain some new friends. I've noticed that my study group friends are much more open to assisting each other than regular friends are; we seem to feel each others' needs more. Perhaps it's because we've come together under the Lord's hand, maybe it's because we're just reaching out to each other as the Lord commanded. I'm not sure; I just know that I give as much as I can to assisting these guys in times of need. I guess there's a special bonding there.

Before making a decision to join any group that meets on a regular basis, you will need to schedule your time to attend the meetings. Sometime we truly wish to join, but fail to see that we won't be able to make the meetings as required. So with a heart full of good intensions, we join, only to fall away after a few months or so, and then we feel that we have failed. In today's age, we find that our time is governed by so many different responsibilities that there isn't enough time to go around. So be careful when joining these study groups.

Making this move towards Christ is a wonderful thing, however, we don't want to overextend ourselves and then feel as if we have failed to make the connection. Some folks have the ability to be available for most of the events that take place, and others, such as I, just don't. I could, perhaps, have made more time available to join in some activities, but haven't. Again, I stress that connecting to Jesus is an individual thing. Our Lord is very pleased with us when we begin to seek him out. So do so. Getting help along this journey is wonderful, but the drive must come from our hearts. We must walk this path physically on our own, but spiritually with Jesus.

* * * *

I'M NOT SURE JUST HOW I came up with this piece. I awoke one morning at about 1 AM, and what stuck in my head was the question, "What do the gates of heaven look like?" With that question in my mind, I couldn't return to restful slumber, so I started thinking and with that …

THE GATES OF HEAVEN

There are so many paths
To walk in our lives,
It's hard to know if decisions made
Have been done right,
If we just hold on to our faith,
We'll always walk in the light.

The gates of heaven, the gates of heaven
Are they golden? Are they iron?
Are they made of steel?
When we pass through them,

How shall we feel?
Oh, how I long to see
The gates of heaven.

Through the years as we walk,
Following our Lord,
Fighting off the darkness
With love as our sword,
Though we lose more than we win
We never become bored.

As we know, we'll get to

The gates of heaven. The gates of heaven.
Are they golden? Are they iron?
Are they made of steel?
When we pass through them,
How shall we feel?
Oh how I long to see
The gates of heaven.

Comes our time
One faithful day,
We'll see the light
And find our way,
And hear our Lord say,
"My child, it's time to come home."

And then we'll see

The gates of heaven. The gates of heaven.
Are they golden? Are they iron?
Are they made of steel?

When we pass through them,
How shall we feel?
Oh how I long to see
The gates of heaven.

Chapter Eight
Jesus Is Everywhere

I'VE OFTEN THOUGHT ABOUT where Jesus dwells. Does he only dwell in heaven, sitting upon his throne and watching us all? I don't really know for sure—none of us do—but I have an idea. Perhaps he is within us. Perhaps his spirit or essence is living inside us, waiting for us to recognize the fact that he's right here.

I know that when I pray to him, I sometimes get the feeling that the hairs on the back of my neck are standing up, and I just know it's him. It's a sense that he's here with me, feeling my hurts, needs, and wants. He knows what I'm going through because he is a part of me, and my feelings are his. You see, we are one, just as Margie and I are one.

The Lord and I are also one, but on a different plain. This is very difficult to explain. Some folks will think that I've lost my mind, but I can assure you that I haven't. I've only lost a few marbles!! All kidding aside, I do feel him; it's as though he speaks to me. When I know I need to follow through on something that needs to be done but am putting it off, Jesus is there to prompt me, to gently nudge me along. He keeps me on the right road, and I'm learning to work with him, to listen more carefully to his words.

I must admit, the hardest thing to do when dealing with Jesus is to confess that we are a broken race. We humans are flawed, and until we can admit that fact with all honesty, we will have a hard time dealing with the teachings of Jesus. When you let go and face this fact, then the walls come down and healing begins. Yes, my friends, we are so stubborn to think that we are in complete control.

Control is a word that should be removed from our vocabulary. There is only one who is in control; I've come to believe that with all my heart. As I begin to remove the blinders that I've worn for so many years, I see all the brokenness in our world. No matter how much we may say we don't believe in God, when times get tough, he's the first one we turn to.

Jesus also indicated that we were an unbelieving nation, and he was so right. Could it be that we do believe because we know? The fact that God has put his laws in our minds already should tell us he's real, but we're hiding this belief because we don't want anyone to point a finger at us; we just want to blend into society.

This could be, but perhaps what we need to do is look at society. Yes, if we actually look at those folks that are right here with us, I think we'll see Jesus. We'll see him in their eyes, their actions, their love and devotion for helping in his name. When Jesus went to the cross to die for us, not only did it hurt and still does hurt to think of it, he actually be*came* us. With his death, he brought life to us all. Jesus's spirit has passed from one frail human body to that of all God's children. I know that he lives in me.

Think of this. If Jesus lives in you, and you love him, then you must love yourself. Going one step further, if he lives in all of us, no matter who we are, then we must love each other for we all are one. This is the whole point of his teachings. No one is better than his brother; we are all the same. A human is nothing more than that, a human. No matter how we dress, speak, our education level, our monetary gains, none of this matters; it doesn't change us at all, we are still human. We are the children of God, and we should be proud to bear that distinction.

I remember the story of Jesus, the greatest living being on our planet, washing the feet of his disciples; he did this to prove that no one is greater than his brother. Love must come from the heart with truth and honesty, love knows no boundaries; it has no borders; it contains no lies. For love, we must stoop to whatever level is necessary to help those in need. Love is not only what Jesus taught us; it's what he gave us when he died on the cross. His essence and his love were then instilled in all of humanity. It resides locked up in our hearts, and only we have the key to unlock its power.

Love is true power, it out-shines the brightest stars; it reaches past the farthest horizons the eye can see, and it brings hope to those without hope. Jesus made disciples of all of us; he has given us power far beyond our knowledge; he has entrusted us with his love. Now it is for us to understand this and use this gift from our Lord to give back hope, life, and love to our brothers in need. Each and every one of us is Jesus; we are his hands, arms, feet, eyes and ears, we are his heart; we are the love of Jesus.

*　　*　　*　　*

WHILE IN BIBLE STUDY, I began thinking of how many times we say, "Where is Jesus?" I guess we expect him to just show up one day and say, "Hi, my name is Jesus!" Well, I think we see him all the time in everyday life, in everyday people. We just need to open our eyes and see him there. In my writings, I always say that his essence is within all of us, and that from some, it shines like a bright light. We walk around so lost in our own problems and burdens that we don't see it. With this all said, I heard the call to write once again.

WHERE IS JESUS?

Every day we search for Jesus.
We wonder where He'll be.

Will we find Him on a mountain top,
Or will He be sitting next to me?

Do we need to visit His tomb?
Or find Him at the cross.
I keep asking Him to come to me,
But I am one of the many who are lost.

Where is Jesus? When can we see?
I keep searching. Where can He be?
In the faces of my brothers whom
I worship with and pray?
We are the body of Christ.
I've found Jesus this very day.

When I see the young and old
Entwined in wondrous love,
I see my Lord and Savior,
His majesty shining from above

The homeless on the streets
With no place to lay their heads.
These are the *words* of Jesus
Just as scripture has said.

Where is Jesus so that we may see?
I keep searching; where can He be?
In the faces of my brothers whom
I worship with and pray.
We are the body of Christ.
I've found Jesus this very day.

Volunteers who share their time,
Many more who bear the burden

They have within their souls.
The essence of this is Jesus,
I am certain.

For those who have a love of life,
Their hands dedicated to healing,
And those who go into the world
To share the word and feeling.

Where *is* Jesus? When can we see?
I keep searching. Where can He be?
In the faces of my brothers whom
I worship with and pray.
We are the body of Christ.
I've found Jesus this very day.

Lord Jesus, my savior, my God
I have begun to understand,
Though you dwell in a land beyond,
Your soul can still be found in man

As I look to the heavens,
I begin to see
That you, my Lord,
Are still within me.

Where is Jesus? When can we see?
I keep searching. Where can He be?
In the faces of my brothers whom
I worship with and pray.
We are the body of Christ.
I've found Jesus this very day

Chapter Nine
A Life of Death

I OFTEN THINK OF WHAT a horrible creation I am. I ask Jesus to accept me into his heart, and I try to follow his word, but then turn around and fail to follow through. The key word here is *fail*. We have all gone through this cycle of events, so I know I'm not alone here. But still, that fact doesn't change what I've done and how disgusted I have become with myself. I feel as if Jesus should turn from me and cast me aside. Yet he never does. When I pray to him each morning, he hears me. He feels my pains, needs, cares, and answers them time and time again. How loving and forgiving he is. I imagine that after spending thirty plus years with us on this planet, he truly did find us worthy to die for. He saw in us a beauty that we'll never see in ourselves, for we are blinded by our own evil.

The amazing thing is, although we are such evil beings, we still have the ability to create such beauty. Beauty in writings, song, music, artistry, architecture, etc. We have the beauty from God's hand—all of nature, all that lives on our planet. I couldn't even begin to call off the long list of life that Earth supports, everything from flowers and trees to birds, fish, insects and such. Think not only of what now exists on our planet, but also about those species that have died off—like the dinosaurs.

And talk about beauty. How about the oceans of the world and all of the natural wonders? We can't even begin to absorb his gifts to us. We walk right by the most beautiful tree on our way to the store; we look but never see it. It's just an object to us. It takes too much time to stop and smell the roses. We just walk right by, ignoring their existence.

Sound familiar to you? *Is* this you? Well, my friends, we do this not only to trees and flowers, but to our fellow humans as well. Yes, our own kind. How many times have you crossed the street to avoid the homeless man or the bag lady? How many times have we walked past the veteran who is collecting for the disabled vets who fought for us? How many times have we failed to drop in some loose change to help feed the hungry? Many times more than we could count. So how can beings like ourselves, who can create such beauty, yet be so cold, ask for forgiveness from Jesus, and expect to get it? I truly don't have an answer for this one, because I have failed just as badly as you.

I can only search through the Bible and try to understand the teaching of our Lord. I have hope that Jesus will forgive my sins as I try to understand the laws of God, that which he has put within me. Jesus understands us better than we understand ourselves. Perhaps it's the guilt we feel that becomes our punishment when we fail to live up to those laws that we cast aside. That guilt has a way of lingering, of torturing our souls. Even if we are not believers in God, it still haunts us.

I once saw a ring, and on it was written a word. Picking up the ring and reading from one perspective, I saw the word, "Life." But turning it over, that same word read "Death."

Life and Death—two opposites, yet one in the same. You see, we can live our lives in death by not seeing the beauty around us. We are, in essence, killing ourselves. If we can open up and begin to see this beauty, then we will live a better life. Death then becomes nothing more than a doorway to a new life with the Lord. So now even death gives us life.

The beauty of God's creation can be summed up in one small word—HOPE. His beauty is all around us and within us. Hope is there for all who can find it within themselves to reach for it.

* * * *

MY INSPIRATION FOR MY POEM, "Sounds of Heaven," came while I was sitting on my front porch with a cup of coffee. It was early morning, and I had closed my eyes for just a moment, drinking in the start of a new day. While my eyes were closed, I started to notice all the sounds around me and just how beautiful they were.

Different sounds have different meanings to different people, but no matter what the sound or meaning, they all lead back to the beauty of God's creation and the love that comes with it.

SOUNDS OF HEAVEN

In the early morning hours
As I stand one with nature,
I feel a touch of love
That comes only from my Maker.

I open my ears
To the rustling of the trees.
I hear the whisper of the wind;
It's the song of the breeze.

These are the sounds of heaven
That man can hear on earth.
The beauty of God's creation
Given to us at birth.

It's a symphony of beauty.
These are the sounds of heaven.

The cry of a baby,
Laughter of a child,
The sigh of an old friend,
The call of the wild.

Hear the gurgling of a brook,
The crashing of the waves,
The whisper of your love.
It's Him who came to save.

These are the sounds of heaven
That man can hear on earth,
The beauty of God's creation
Given to us at birth.
It's a symphony of beauty.
These are the sounds of heaven

Listen to the silence of winter,
The crackling of a fire.
God's love comes in many forms,
So many we'll never tire.

The falling of the rain,
Song's of the dove.
When we open up our senses,
We hear our Lord's cry of love.

These are the sounds of heaven
That man can hear on earth.
The beauty of God's creation
Given to us at birth.

It's a symphony of beauty.
These are the sounds of heaven.

Chapter Ten
The Promise

EACH DAY BRINGS WITH IT new challenges that can stretch our abilities to the limits. We can learn much about ourselves through these ordeals. When we walk alone, we are apt to question ourselves and begin to lose confidence. This is when the power of darkness slowly begins to weave itself into the picture. You see, that feeling of being alone allows a crack to open up, and this is all the fallen ones need to help us fail.

Yes, the fallen ones, the evil ones, the Devil; it does not matter what you call them—they are there. Jesus and his league of angels are always at odds with the bad guys; it's the standard battle between good and evil. We know it exists; it exists on a human level as well as a spiritual level. So when that crack opens up, the dark side goes for it, and like a wedge, these evil beings push in and split us wide open. They fill us with doubt, uncertainty, and they rattle us right to the bone so much that we fail. Then they whisper to us that God can't be real, that there is no Jesus, since, if there were, he would have helped us. So in tearing us down, they are trying to pull us from our faith, and this is how they become stronger.

At one time I thought of faith as being "blind faith." Blind, meaning that we don't see God or Jesus before us in the flesh; we don't hear either the Father or the Son talking to us, but we're asked to believe in them. Well, I was so wrong. God and Jesus *are* here, we *do* see them, or perhaps I should say, we see their beauty; their essence is all around us. We hear them speak to us by their love and their devotion. Their voice is the wind, and that voice can be a gentle whisper or a gale force roar. We just fail to understand this. I believe that we are all tied together; the good being our Lord Jesus, the bad being the powers of darkness, and the lost being us humans!

God created all of us. Some naturally follow Christ, for they are drawn to him early on. Others, for some reason, stay lost and just don't realize that Jesus is there, so they wind up going down the wrong path and fall into darkness. The remaining, who are lost just seem to wander, not realizing what path to take.

This is where the battleground lies. Good and Evil clash here where the lost dwell. This sounds like a great science fiction movie, but broken down into simple terms, this is just what is happening. It's been going on for centuries. What is so disturbing is that it isn't hidden from us. All this takes place in full view of the entire world, and some of us are so blind to it all.

I titled this chapter "The Promise" because I wanted to bring out the point that following Jesus isn't a one-way street. He asks a lot of us, but there is a wonderful return on our investment. Before I go into the promise of Jesus, let's look at what the other side has to offer.

The Devil in his dark world offers us power, riches, lust, and a never-ending greed for more. Sounds just like what most of us want, doesn't it? Think of it, never having to want for anything, having money to burn, so to say. People looking up to us and saying, "I wish I could be like that." "Why, we'll be superstars." Heck, why not go for such a lifestyle?

Well, it is a great offer, but there's one little catch, as far as I can see, which is simply that you lose your soul. You now belong to them. You see, you now have become addicted to all this power and money and such; you need it, and you can't live without it; like a drug, you're hooked ... period!! You have now lost you soul, your honor, your self-esteem; you, in essence, have lost what life is all about. You probably have also lost the ones who care about you, friends and family, wife and children, and—the way it may look to you—the worst of it is that now the only one who can help you is Jesus. Yes, Jesus. Remember? The fellow you've been cursing and ignoring? The one who has nothing you need? It sure hurts to think that he can help you now.

Well he can, Jesus, the Christ, the Son of Man, the Son of God—call him what you will, he is the only one who can help you, and he will. His help comes at a cost, though. What's the cost? It's simple, your belief in him; you have to open the door to your heart. You have to love him and let him guide you back to life. You see, he has already taken care of the hard part; he gave his life for you, he let himself be nailed to a wooden cross and die. This was done for all mankind, but also for you, for he loves you as a brother, because you *are* his brother. There is nothing more one can do for another then give his life—or hers. This is the most precious thing we have.

So remember this, my friend, no matter how deep you fall into the pit of darkness, no matter how hard those evil beings try to grab on, when you call to Jesus for help, he'll be there, and those bad guys will turn and run, because they have no love, and they do not care for you.

The only true power is love, and that's what Jesus has; he is the light, and light cuts through the darkness like a hot knife cuts through butter. If you want real power and riches, turn from the darkness and walk with Jesus.

The promise of Jesus is simple; this is my interpretation of it. He will never leave you. When you're in need of help, he will help even if it means carrying you until you can stand on your own again. His love will never leave you; his guidance will always be there for you. He will provide for you not in abundance, but you will never be without. Yes, times may get hard but you will survive. You see, we humans don't need much to live; but we're used to having more than what we need. Jesus will provide us with what we need, but will shower us with all of his love.

There is no greed and there are no power struggles in his kingdom. There is long, healthy life with much friendship and love. You're not hooked as if on a drug, in the way you might have been while dwelling in the darkness. You have honor, freedom, and self-esteem; you have life. One of the best features of his promise is that—although our loved ones will pass on and the loss hurts—we'll be reunited in his kingdom. So with all this hanging in the balance, the choice is yours and it's a simple one; live for life or live in death.

* * * *

THE FEELINGS OF LONELINESS are not foreign to most of us. One may find their soul mate early on, another at a later time, and unfortunately, some never do. My thought in this poem centered on the waves of emotion upon losing a mate, going from a state of bliss, to heartbreak, to hate, to confusion, to not even wanting to live. How does one come to terms with moving on? Is it truly better to have loved a short time than never having loved?

What are our inner feelings and dealings with Christ at these times? Will we turn from him in dismay? Will we hold onto our faith, or will we say, "I remember Your Promise."

YOUR PROMISE

I live the life You asked me to.
I followed the teachings that came from You.
I gave of my life and all I had,
Yet the loneliness I felt made me very sad.

In Your name I prayed and told of my strife.
From my heart came this request, bring to me someone to share my life
The fire in my heart You did not douse.
You searched the world over and gave me the perfect spouse.

Your promise to help me, to guide me, to love me
Are words shown to be true, for this I cannot help but love You.
Lord, You have given to me someone to share;
For this I thank You. You truly do care.

For years we did walk, step by step, hand in hand.
Our lives intertwined like highways across the land.
Through the years our love grew, and two became one.
This all came true because of You, the Father's son.

For years we grew, never once torn or tattered,
Until that day when my life was truly shattered.
The words that I heard showed my heart had been severed.
My love had been taken from me—gone forever.

Being brought to my spouse, I could not bear to say good-bye.
I could only hold her cold lifeless hand, bow my head, and cry.

Your promise to help me, to guide me, to love me,
Are words shown to be true, for this I cannot help but love You.
But for a short time my love turned to dismay,
As I could not understand how You could leave me this way

Once again I was alone, lost more now than before.
I saw the light dim and darkness shutting the door.

My life had no meaning. I was willing to let it go,
Until my spouse spoke to me, "Remember, you reap what you sow"

With her words of love reaching my heart,
I fought for my life to gain a new start.
Though she is not here, and neither are You,
The love I have for both is still alive and true.

Each night before I sleep, I close my eyes and my spouse I kiss.
For I will be with her again; in my heart I hold Your promise

Your promise to help me, to guide me, to love me
Are words shown to be true, for this I cannot help but love You.
Although I do not understand why my love had to go,
In the kingdom of God we'll again walk hand in hand—of this I know.

Chapter Eleven
The Death of a King

EACH OF US HAS WONDERED what it would be like to be a king or a queen. We think of all the riches and honors that would be bestowed on us. How we would dress so eloquently and dine with only the most honored guests. The cheering crowds, the wide-eyed children gazing upon us as we moved about. Oh, how wonderful it would be to live in a palace adorned with fine paintings and lavish tapestries. Oh, what a life we would have.

Now, let's go a few steps farther. Think of our Lord Jesus Christ. No one could deny that his status, although we call him a king, goes far beyond that which we understand or could ever imagine. Would we desire to be like him? I think most of us who believe in him would say, "Yes, I would like to be just like Jesus."

We think of all his knowledge, love, powers of healing, the miracles that he performed; all of this is wonderful and it brings joy to our hearts to think of it. But have we thought about this? What it would be like if we knew—as he did—that someone is going to die, and that even though we have the power to heal, we can't, for life and nature must progress with some normality. If miracles were performed everyday, then they would lose the status of miracle. How about watching a loved child struggle for life, knowing that you could bring them health, but again, having to hold back, for the processes of life and death must go on.

Consider watching a family being torn apart by abuse or drugs, and again, having to restrain yourself. You see, Jesus can do many wonderful things, and I believe he does them when he can, but because of our evil nature and the downfall of man in the Garden of Eden, we must suffer; we must struggle to learn just how precious life is, and in this, we must learn that the balance of nature must be kept in order to keep our world life-sustaining.

We parents want to give our children all that they need to make a success of themselves in life, but they must *want* to be successful. Giving to them is necessary, but they must develop and mature on their own; they must be able to stand on their own feet and move ahead when we are gone. If our children don't have the desire or drive to mature, then no matter how much we give them, they will fail.

We, the children of God, have failed and continue to fail because we will not accept the responsibility to become mature. Just as we lay down the rules for our children, God has laid down his rules for us, and even though we know of them, we often cast them aside as though they mean nothing to us. We sometimes show no respect and simply ignore him, just as children ignore the teachings of their parents.

So Jesus struggles with how best to help us, and sometimes this means letting us stray off course and get into troubled water. Hopefully, this leads us to opening our minds to his presence, for when in trouble, who do we always call to?

Again, we want to make things better for our children, but there are times when we must hold back and let them hurt so that they will understand that we only want to help them. And so it is for God.

We make our own troubles. We are a stubborn creation, but perhaps one day we'll learn. Perhaps we'll understand that being a king, especially the type of king that our Lord is, goes further than just being powerful and smart; it goes further than being a loving being or a loved one. It means giving of yourself to those that need you even if it means losing face as Jesus did when he was questioned and beaten and spat upon by those who, by comparison to him, were so insignificant. Even if it means being wrongly accused, as Jesus was wrongly accused of blasphemy when he announced that he was the Son of God.

Giving of yourself means to freely give your life, such a precious thing, for those that you love. You do it to protect them, to help them, to show your love for them.

I can't emphasize enough that Jesus took human form so that the people of that time would not fear him as they feared the God in heaven. He did this so the people would better understand him. Jesus, who knew all and who could have lived here on earth with us for much longer than he did, gave his life for us with little thought for himself.

Jesus knew quite well just what was going to happen to him. He knew the pain and indignity that he was to bear, and he knew how he was going to suffer while not only being nailed to the cross but hanging there and dying a slow death, literally baking in the sun. Most of us hope for a quick and painless death, and we do not want to know when and how it is to happen.

This king knew it all, and even though he had the choice to turn and walk away, he didn't. Jesus knew what was to come, and he went when the time came. There was no kicking or screaming; there was no denial of his love for us. With each blow to the face, with each spit in the face, with each pounding of the nails, his love shone through. Yes, my friends, Jesus did love us with all his heart, with all his soul, and he gave of himself.

Now, I ask you again, would you like to be like Jesus? Would you like to bear the burdens that he bore for us? Are you willing to give your life for the entire world? Can you willingly allow yourself to be nailed to a cross and die for such broken people? I would never have the courage that he did. When I think of what his life must have been like, it makes me bow my head and cry. For this man, this king, this

God, I would do whatever he asks of me. I may fall often on the journey with Jesus, but I'll never stop following him or loving him.

* * * *

I AWOKE ONE EVENING with this on my mind and couldn't stop thinking about it until I wrote it.

UPON MY CROSS

I have been before creation,
Before you were, I gave my love
Yet you chose to go astray.
You ignored the teaching from above.

You have felt the pain of sin.
Yet you dwell within the darkness.
I have tried to light your path,
Yet you turned from my kiss.

I have heard your cries for help.
I have come to heal your wounds.
I will walk the path of glory,
Though it will lead me to eventual doom.

Upon my cross
I shall hang
With love for all.
The angels have sang.
I gave my life;
For you I die, and
For the Fathers glory.
So do not cry.

Just see me hang
Upon my cross.

My teachings are hard
But true of heart.
I came to bind,
Not break apart.

I am a king
Who comes to you,
To the people of Israel,
For Gentile and Jew.

There are those who will love me
And those who will hate.
They want to see my power,
But my love is far too great.

Upon my cross
I shall hang
With love for all.
The angels have sang.
I gave my life,
For you I die,
For the Fathers glory.
So do not cry,
Just see me hang
Upon my cross.

My time had come; I was arrested.
Shackled and bound, I stood in place.
They questioned and hit me,
Then they spit in my face.

They brought me to trial.
They wanted me to die.
The judge wanted mercy,
But my people cried "Crucify."

I was beaten again
And called a false king.
I walked to my death,
Yet my heart still did sing.

As I was nailed to the cross,
The pain did not matter.
For in a short time
The curtain would shatter.

Upon my cross
I shall hang
With love for all.
The angels have sang.
I gave my life.
For you I die
For the Father's glory.
So do not cry;
Just see me hang
Upon my cross.

When I was placed to rest within my tomb,
They all cried—those who called me friend.
Little did they understand
That I was to rise again.

On the third day I did indeed
Walk the Earth upon my feet.

My wounds still there for all to see,
My words were true for thee to seek.

Upon the mountain on Galilee,
My words were written upon the page.
I am surely with you always,
To the very end of the age.

Upon my cross
I shall hang.
Just see me hang
Upon my cross.

Chapter Twelve
An Empty Presence

THE MORE TIME I SPEND with Jesus, the more I learn of what his teachings mean. I've found that what we think of as being successful truly isn't. All, the wants of life are simply not needed. Keeping up with the neighbor's game is foolish indeed. The waste of time and resources is huge. We are so blinded by our greed that we lose sight of the most important thing given to us—life.

My friend, life is so precious and delicate that the only thing that can nurture it is the gift of love. We cast love aside as though it were a sheet of paper. The loss of love is hurting us so badly. We, as a people, should be proud to say that we can love and feel love for one another, but in our society we are often ashamed to say the words, "I love you." Some even think it's dirty, wrong, and bad. How warped is that thought? Love is a beautiful thing; we must never forget that. Love is why Jesus came to this world; it's why he walked with us and taught us. It's why he died for us. And that is another thing that we must never forget.

So how do we make sure we remember?

First, we must teach ourselves to understand this, and then we must teach our children to understand. Only *we* can change the future; it is in our power to do so. I say this because God could have just destroyed the Earth and started again, but he didn't. He came to earth as Jesus to show us our faults, to guide us along, to give of himself and demonstrate the power of love. For centuries he has watched over us, cared for us, given us hope. He was always there, is there now, and will be there for all the ages.

His hand is upon us, his love is within our hearts, and we need to tap into it. We have beaten ourselves into a corner and built a brick wall in order to protect ourselves. But who *should* we fear? Well, ourselves. We are the evil ones. We keep hurting ourselves, yet here we are trapped behind this brick wall! Break it down, break it down, my friends; that wall is keeping us from the glory of God.

Remember, *we* built the wall, *we* cornered ourselves, and only *we* can bring the wall down and walk out of that corner.

There are no excuses, simply listen to *yourself*. That inner voice is God talking; don't ignore it, don't ignore him. Feel the love, give the love, and *say* that you love. This is a gift without bounds; it can fuel the fire of life; it brings a tear to the eye. Love is a powerful thing. It was entrusted to us, and we only need to learn how to use it properly.

You see, we know God is with us. This is engrained in our being, planted there by God himself when he formed us. That seed wants to sprout, it needs to sprout, but it requires love for it to start growing. It is the cold of heart who wander the wastelands of emptiness and loneliness. But for those who can grasp the word of our Lord Jesus and open their hearts, these are the ones who let the love flow and pass from the emptiness into the light. The love that dwells within grows from a burning ember to a raging inferno, an inferno that burns away the darkness, the loneliness, and brings life to a once empty soul.

An empty soul is something I remember having. All my material possessions meant nothing to me. They brought no happiness, no contentment. Even my smile was empty, my heart lost and yearning for something; I just couldn't understand what I needed. It took many years for me to begin to breakdown that wall I had built to protect myself. So many wasted years to learn that I had unknowingly turned my back on Jesus. But that was ok; he knew that I had to do that. I needed to learn what I was doing to myself, and I had to learn it the hard way. To be perfectly honest, that is how I learn best!!

Please, my friends, don't be like me. Don't waste years of your life wandering and searching for the thing that is right in front of your face, or—better put—right in your own heart. Take it from me; there is nothing to be scared of, nothing to fear. Jesus, the Christ, the Savior, knows our deepest feelings, fears, and needs. He is there waiting for us to simply say, "please help me find my way; I am lost and broken. I need you to hold me and show me how to love and be loved."

That is all there is to it. Once you can learn to love him and trust him, then you'll begin to feel different.

Slowly, the light will begin to shine. There is no doubt about it; your life will change, and it will change for the better.

Please allow me to give you the hope to continue on. Don't let the darkness take over and cloud your thoughts to the point that you find yourself feeling that there is no hope left. Believe me, this can happen and has. So many wonderful people have taken their own lives because they thought that no one cared about them.

Let me say that you are my brother or my sister, even though we have never met and may never meet. We are all one in the body of Jesus. My love for you is real. I have been on the road that you now walk. Come with me; come to Jesus. Break the cold heart. Let the love flow. Water that seed, and let the light of Jesus Christ shine on you to light your way, to warm your heart. Join me on a wondrous walk along a path of love and true freedom. Let us journey together.

* * * *

I WAS IN THE YARD ON THE DECK having a cup of morning coffee and gazing at a lonely tree standing firm off in the distance. I watched as its leaves, which had now turned various colors and become curled and hard, fall to the ground. This, signaling the coming of winter. I thought of how that tree must feel, losing its beloved leaves and having to let go.

My thoughts turned to how I felt watching my little girl blossom into a beautiful young woman. I thought of the heartaches of having to let her go to find herself, and realized that even while letting her go, I can hold on to our special relationship, and that it will continue to grow always.

A Tree of Torn Hearts

As I lazily gaze at the tree
Standing so proudly in the yard,
Its limbs still reaching skyward,
Its once green leaves now curled and hard,

I see within myself
A heart once filled with life
Only to find itself now
Being cut to pieces with time's knife.

I watch as the wind
Whips through the branches.
I see the leaves fall to the ground
As though performing glorious dances.

My heart once beat proudly,
Feeling full and in total control.
Now as time quickly passes,
My heart weeps and looks to be consoled.

That proud tree once stood
Tall in all of its glories,

Giving of itself to those that needed.
And now it's naked, bare, lonely not yet past its forties.

Although my heart may be torn
By the natural progression of time,
The love that dwells within it
Will never cease to shine.

The leaves may fall away,
And coldness will come again.
Be assured the love of nature
Will once again fill the bare tree in.

Although time has done its damage,
My heart will never fail.
The savior knows no boundaries;
He will once again set my heart to sail.

Chapter Thirteen
A Torn Heart

OH, THE PAIN IN writing this chapter. What lies written here comes from the depths of my own heart. For those of us who have families, the choices we must make in order to serve both God and family are so incredibly difficult to execute. It's written in scripture that no one can serve two masters, both God and money. They will love the one and despise the other.

So my question to Jesus is, "If I'm to put you first, then does that mean my family has to come second?"

Now, through all my life I was taught that family does come first—especially the immediate family, spouse, and children. So how am I to serve God and family all at the same time? There have been many instances where I wanted to put in some—I'll call it "Jesus time." Possibly meaning going to church or volunteering or something of that nature. But many times I decided not to do that, but, instead, to put the time into my family.

Although I chose them over God, I wasn't sure that they really appreciated the time I was giving them. Did they care that I was pushing away my newfound friend in Jesus? Did they know how much this relationship with Jesus meant to me? I felt that I was letting God down.

But perhaps I wasn't. I was taking care of my family; isn't that why God gave me a family? Isn't it expected for me to take care of them, to love them and spend time with them?

This is a big sticking point between Jesus and me. Needless, to say, it has been mentioned many times in church that we are to put God first. And it's written in the Bible. My love for God is strong, but I stand my ground. I'm on firm footing when I say that my responsibility is to my wife and daughter first, and then I give whatever I can to God. What sometimes hurts so much is that one's family may expect you to devote time to them and nothing else; they lose sight of your feelings.

Many people will not like what I have said here, that my family should come first, but I cannot deviate from what is in my heart. Yes, God can better provide for my family with all the power that he has and all his love. Yes, he can better provide, *but he can never replace me.* Even if he were to come to Earth and physically be here for my family, he would never be able to replace me, for the power of love—the love that he has given to us humans—is so strong that my family would always have an emptiness within for me when I'm gone from them. My love for them goes so deep within my soul that I would not hesitate to give my life for them. Again, isn't this what Jesus did for us? He gave his life because he loved us?

On the one hand, I'm trying to care for my family as best I can. These are such trying times, I need to be diligent to be there for them—even if they don't appreciate it. I must go above and beyond in order to be sure that the foundation I build for them is solid and will stand the test of the most difficult times.

On the other hand, I'm trying to understand what is expected of me from a spiritual standpoint. I know I must give my life to Jesus, to believe in him. And I do. I truly try to listen to his words and teaching. However, I can never forsake my wife or daughter. These two are the most precious things that I have. They were a blessing from the Lord, and I will put them before all to ensure they are cared for. God knows this. I truly believe that this is one very large test for us.

When we seek to find him and understand him, we need to put into perspective what he asks of us. We are his children, and as such, he gives all of himself to care for us, and I believe it is expected of us to do the same for our families.

Some may say that God gave his son for us and we should do the same. I disagree, and please try to understand my stance here; in my view, God and Jesus are, in essence, one in the same. Jesus was God in human form. He gave of *himself* for us. God was willing to give his own life for us. The parent was willing to give his life for his children. My giving first to my family is, in essence, the same. Giving one's life is an extreme case, but we are willing to do so if necessary.

The point I'm trying to make here is not to question what was written in the Bible, but to better understand our responsibilities and what is expected of us. We are God's family; there is no question on that point. We come first to him; he wants the best for us, and he goes far above and beyond to teach us and to be patient. I believe that we are expected to do the same. Did Jesus not say, "Be ye therefore perfect, even as your Father in heaven is perfect"? I'm trying to do the best I can, I realize that I am a broken person; I tell Jesus this every day when I pray to him. I always ask that he help me to do what is right, to help me understand. It's always difficult to choose between the two. My love for both is strong. I believe that being there for my family and loving them with all my heart is, in essence, loving God just the same and doing what is expected of me in his eyes.

For some time now, I've felt that I was falling away from faith, since I had taken so much time away from God to put into my family. I struggled with the torment of being unfaithful to God or to my family, and if I am being unfaithful, does serving God mean casting all to the wind? Oh, how troubling it can be.

It took me a long time to realize that doing what was in my heart and listening to the inner voice of Jesus was what I needed. Through this troubling time, I wrote the poem "Falling from Faith." It embodies all of the feelings I was going through.

FALLING FROM FAITH

Oh Jesus, sweet Jesus, please help me
As I've slipped from your embrace.
As I fall reach down and catch me,
And then shower me with your grace.

I don't disbelieve in you.
I've just drifted, perhaps slightly severed.
You still reside in my heart,
And I need your love now more than ever.

I've given all to my loved ones here.
To give to them I've pushed *us* apart.
And they've returned my love
With a coldness of heart.

Oh Lord, perhaps I've been wrong.
Perhaps I've done too much in the name of love.
Oh Father, I fear I'm slipping, falling from faith into a dark pool.
Your love remains in my heart.
I've done what I thought best, but perhaps I've been a fool.

As I slipped from you, Lord
My life once again became empty.

The loneliness, the anger, the frustration—
They all came at me as one entity.

It was an overwhelming force, one to behold.
I was beaten—I crumbled—I fell,
My strength taken from me, my world crushed.
I felt I was on a fast train to hell.

Love can be wonderful, yet can cut to the bone.
It can lift us high or drop us into a dark pit.
Love is one of the greatest gifts you've given us,
Yet it can throw us into a raging fit.

Please Lord, stop the shaking, stop the falling.
Catch me, raise me up and hold me to your breast.
Make the hurt stop—
Give me the chance to rest.

Oh Father, I fear I'm slipping,
Falling from faith. I'm loosing my sight.
Please Lord, help me.
Don't let me lose the fight.

I am so sorry for letting the world get the best of me.
Perhaps my folly was in trying to make the grade,
For without you there is no light,
No freedom, no true love, just gray—a lonely shade.

In this time of despair, I pray to you.
I ask your love, understanding, and guidance.
And from your lips come words of hope,
Words of love and words of truth, not silence.

Lord Jesus, I may have slipped and fallen slightly away.
But I have not lost you; no I will never give you up.
For I will always remember that you died for me.
You loved me so much; you drank from the cup.

The pain you suffered was far more than I could endure.
Of this I know, I will never let you fade from my life—yes,
of this I'm sure.

Chapter Fourteen
A Deep Rooted Love

IT WON'T COME AS A SURPRISE to you that I sometimes still feel a little lost and lonely. It is at times like these that I listen for that little voice inside of me—you know the one I'm talking about—the one where Jesus speaks to me and tells me that he is there, that he hasn't left me. He still loves me—even if I am a total disaster! The thing to remember is that I need to open my ears and listen for him.

Feelings of loneliness are like the cold, bony fingers of death. They slowly creep into my inner soul, and when I least expect it, they grab hold of my heart and squeeze with all their might. Their goal is to remove every last drop of love, compassion, and self-esteem. If they were to accomplish this, then I would be only an empty shell, and the loneliness would fill me and overtake reason. I would become lost and frustrated, and perhaps become an empty void and lose sight of life, for there would seem to be nothing to live for.

I think it must be in times like these that ones so precious to us take their own lives. We are at a loss to understand this. But we must make no mistake about it; loneliness is a very strong force—it comes from the evil one, the sly Devil that he is.

How do we combat this? Well, we must never lose faith that Jesus loves us. He is always there; he knows the trials and tribulations that we go through. We must remember that he lived here on Earth with us, was one of us, and that this is how he knows us so well. Jesus has felt all our human emotions and pains.

You and I can never approach Jesus with a situation that he hasn't experienced before. This is why he is so special to me. He is a direct link to my soul, for he understands. So I keep my ears open and listen for his voice, feel his love, and most importantly, I know he is there and that he loves me.

I stay alert to the fact that those bony fingers are trying to sneak into my life, and when I see them, I cut them off! Easy to say but difficult to do. But when I begin to feel a little down or alone, having someone to talk to is a step in the right direction. Some of us are lucky to have many friends to speak with, and others have few or none. But Jesus is my friend. Yes, he is the Lord of all, but he is also my friend. He wants me to be comfortable with him and never to be afraid to talk to him.

It was hard in the beginning to think of a God as my personal friend. Some divine being who cared what I was going through. How can that be when I am so insignificant? Why should he bother with me? And yet, I remember that my God picked a human woman and impregnated her with his essence. The child developed as a normal human would. When born, that child grew and experienced life as any normal child would.

There is so much that we don't know of Jesus's life before he began teaching. I think Mary played a large part in his understanding of human love, for she is the one who was his mother, and she was human. As the woman chosen to bear this child and raise him, Mary was very special.

Remembering this, when I think of Jesus, I don't think of a divine being who is set apart from me, as one who displays an image of being above all. A being that I fear to approach—no. I think of Jesus as being a loving friend, a friend that I can go to any time and talk with. I know that he will not forsake me, that he will not turn from me, and he will not ignore me. His humanity shines through; I see him as a loving person whose smile warms my heart and whose loving hands warm my soul.

This is the image of Jesus that is in my heart. And no one can take that image from me. I don't care what the other side has to offer—it can never be better than Jesus. When those bony fingers of loneliness come to feel for an opening in my heart, they leave me quickly. And they will leave, cut off and stubby to boot!

So I am on my guard because life is difficult. The paths are not always smooth ones. I know that when the wind blows, it's Jesus. When the trees rustle, it's Jesus, and when I hear the whisper in my heart, it's Jesus. It's all Jesus.

* * * *

MY LOVE FOR YOU

My dearest child, hear me. Fear not,
For you are now closer than ever to my heart.
Once you come to me, I will never let you go.
Remember the words of scripture, "You shall reap what you sow."

My love for you is greater than the number of stars in the sky.
It's wider than the universe is vast, and it will never die.
You are my child and *of* me.
For you I gave my son, raised the dead and made the blind see.
All this I did for you
Because I love you.

With the new covenant in place, you knew me from the beginning,
Though you did not know—I was with you through all the sinning,
The ups and downs, the heartaches, the loneliness—I was with you through it all.
I cried with you, I hurt with you; I never left you, not once,
For I am there when you call

From the time of your birth until the day you return home,
Be assured on one thing, you will never walk alone.
Your heart may be hardened or open to me.
It matters not, you see, for you are my child,
And I will always love you.

Chapter Fifteen
Is Love Perfection?

HERE IS A THOUGHT-PROVOKING QUESTION. If we are a broken people, and none of us are perfect, why did God create us like this? God is all-powerful. He can do many things, and he is perfect. Jesus said, "Be ye therefore perfect, even as your Father in heaven is perfect." So God is perfect. So again, I ask, why were we created like this? If God had not given us freewill, then Adam and Eve would not have gone astray in the Garden of Eden. As a result, all would be just fine right now. Is that a correct assumption?

Here's what I think. Had we been denied freewill, then we would not be a perfect creation. With no freewill, we would be nothing more than human robots. God could then program us to do whatever he wanted, and we would follow the programming. There would be no straying from the rules; there would be no breakdown of communications; there would be no emotions, no love.

So just what kind of world would *that* be? I'm not sure if one could love a robot, for it has no love within it to return. It has no real personality, no real sense of right or wrong. It just follows its programming.

So could God love us if we were like that? Isn't the main theme all throughout the Bible, that of love? In order for us to love God, and I mean truly love God as in emotional love, the kind that grips the heart and brings tears to your eyes. This kind of love can't be programmed into someone. It has to be real; it has to be free; it is a part of the freewill package. We are given the opportunity to love or not to love—based on our own individual personalities. This love comes from our hearts; it's an emotion that drives us and can consume us. But it comes from us; it is an emotion, a freewill emotion.

To be perfect, we would need to remove all emotions, those of love, hate, greed, lust, etc. If we did that, we would certainly become quite a bland race. How would we create beauty such as music, paintings, and literature? Don't all these things come from our emotions?

Look at the world that God created; isn't it beautiful in its purest form? When I look at our world, I see the beauty of God—his creativity. All this creativity comes from emotions. His emotions, his heart, and perhaps his freewill. After all, weren't we created in the image of God? I don't think God is a robot, void of all emotion. That isn't what is written in the Bible. God is *full* of emotions, so it stands to reason that he has freewill and that freewill is part of perfection.

I also think this—that perfection is not what we think it is. Our concept of perfect is that nothing goes wrong. There are no breakdowns, no stoppages, no problems; everything just goes, and it all works fine—all the time. That sounds nice, but it isn't real. That's like being tempted with riches. "Look, if you follow me, I'll make you rich and all your problems will go away!" Does this sound familiar? It should, but you and I both know it isn't true, because money isn't the answer to everything.

So our thoughts on perfection are also flawed. Giving us freewill makes us think and gives us that ability to be human and have a personality. It gives us the ability to be beautiful and to create beauty. The beauty comes from love; love is the driving force, just as indicated in the Bible. So love is perfection. Love makes us a perfect creation.

Freewill makes us the perfect creation, but we sometimes choose incorrectly and hurt ourselves by going in the wrong direction. Giving us freewill is like mixing fire and dynamite; this is a very dangerous combination. What can be utilized for good can just as easily turn into disaster.

So with all this said, I must admit I was wrong. It isn't God's fault that we are the way we are. He didn't make us imperfect, he made us perfect by giving us freewill, the ability to choose and to love. By doing this, he made us in his image. That is why we can create such beauty; this is truly a gift from him. If he hadn't given us the freewill to choose, then he would have created a flawed race, and one would be able to say that *he* was imperfect, because he created such an imperfect people.

I often wonder. If God knows all, then he knew that things would get a bit out of hand with us as we developed and matured. We may have come a long way since the caveman, but we still have a very long way to go. It is so reassuring to know that Jesus is there for us to lean on because we can use all the help we can get. Perhaps this is why he gave us Jesus in the first place.

It is a huge responsibility knowing that we were given all that we needed to not only maintain this beautiful world, but to add to its beauty. We have that capability. We can do it, but in order to succeed, we must conquer the—shall I say—control of the freewill factor. The old saying, "You can do it the right way, or you can do it the your way," seems to fit our situation well. We just seem to lean towards doing it the wrong way too often.

So there you have it—a real brain buster question. Is perfection being like robots, or is perfection being "freewilled," loving humans who seem to go down the wrong road more often than not? Perhaps our being imperfect makes us perfect!

✻ ✻ ✻ ✻

"PERFECTION OR LOVE?" is a poem that reflects the question, "Are we an imperfect creation, or is love the perfection which God sought for us?"

PERFECTION OR LOVE?

I can only speak of myself,
For I know not what dwells in others.
My life was empty, barren of you.
It's your light that warms my heart as it does my brothers'.

Before I knew you, Lord
I chased the man, made trinkets.
I longed for love, power, and riches.
But I gave that up to seek you. Who would think it?

Jesus, your teachings are hard but simple.
You ask us to be perfect like the Father.
Yet we are broken and easily misled.
The harder we try, the more we fail, so why bother?

I ask why we are not perfect.
I hate this evil inside of me; what an infliction.
But perhaps in all your knowledge
The essence of love is true perfection.

I think of this because
You, my Lord, are my savior, Jesus.
Willingly you gave your life because you loved us
With a love that has great power and riches.

But perhaps it's my understanding of perfection that is
   flawed.
My faith is solid; it is my humanness that is weak.
Perhaps, just perhaps, the essence of love
Is the perfection I should seek.

Being human, I shall always question.
I will continue to knock, to seek, for this is what you told us.
And I know in my heart that the power and riches of heaven
Can only be found in the love of our savior—you, Jesus.

So I ask the question, love or perfection?
Which is greater, or are they one in the same?
Perhaps *that* is the question.

Chapter Sixteen
Tears of Hope

THE SAYING THAT "sometimes you just want to cry" can be so true. Oh, how many times, as hard as I've tried to help my family, I just seem to run into more and more obstacles, and I begin to break down. You just get the feeling of being overwhelmed, and you really do feel like crying.

It's a hard thing to admit, but I have cried tears of joy and of pain, but lately I've shed tears of hope. Hope that Jesus can help me, guide me, and love me. Hope that there is a future for all of us. Hope that there will *be* a future. It scares me to think that mankind's future could be in the hands of mankind! That would be a disaster.

With all the failures of man, I often wonder how Jesus vents his emotions. What about all the suffering of man? I have always felt that when the rains come, it makes me feel clean and renewed. I just love rainy days. I always remember my mom's saying—"Rainy days mean the dead are happy." Perhaps they—the dead—can see some good on Earth that most of us don't. I like to think of those drops being the tears of Jesus coming to us in the form of rain.

It cleans the air and renews our souls. Maybe the raindrops are tears of sorrow, or maybe they are tears of joy—I'm not sure. I know this, on those rainy days, I get the feeling that I need to walk in the rain, I'm drawn to it. *Can it be that someone or something needs to touch me?*

The act of crying makes me think that I need to stop and try to help that person who is crying; it's like that person is waving a flag asking for help. In hindsight, maybe the flag is being waved not for us to help someone else, but to help ourselves.

There is so much that can be improved upon in our world, and we could certainly do a better job of attending those in need. We still suffer from the infliction of greed, and I'm just as guilty as the next one for not helping more. For the little good I do, there is a lot more waiting to be given. As I indicated before, Jesus has a way of talking to my inner self. I guess it's more like a whisper, but still, when I figure it out, it hits home like a ton of bricks.

I have seen a lot of changes in myself as I journey along this path. One change—I'm a more giving person. But I still need to do more.

We all do, and it shouldn't take horrendous disasters to move us in that direction. It should be a natural thing for us to just help. I never realized how many people had nothing to call their own, and who lived in conditions that I would not even think of as livable. Not until I flew out to the Philippines to visit Margie, my wife. Then I began to realize what folks in other countries were enduring.

The real tragedy here was this—although I understood what was going on, I did not have any real heart for those folks. But I did not have Jesus at that time, so I guess I didn't really *have* a heart. Like the Tin Man in *The Wizard of Oz*, I was an empty shell. You could say that without a heart, we're nothing. Like the Grinch, we're *just plain mean.* I truly hope that after connecting with our Lord and learning to become a real man of God, that I can be remembered as being a guy with a heart. To me, that would be a true honor.

I'm not blessed with wealth. I, like most people, work hard to make ends meet, but I've found that I can squeeze out a few dollars here and there to assist others. The money donated at church goes to keeping programs going to assist those in need. The few coins dropped into various canisters at the market help to keep community programs going and the few dollars donated each month to child support organizations help to give kids a better chance of having a life. The money donated, when broken down, comes to nothing more than coffee money. But it's better spent this way than in the coffee shop in the morning.

So even though it isn't much, it's still something that I'm doing to help someone somewhere. I'm reaching out to help, and that's what Jesus asks us to do in his name. The one thing I haven't done much of is donating my time. That is a tougher thing for me to do. Having a home-based business leaves one open to working all kinds of crazy hours, so that scheduling time to volunteer is very difficult. Just trying to get to church can be a real hurdle at times.

But when we journey with the Lord, he will ask us to help, so we do what we can, no matter how small. Whatever we can do he'll appreciate, and it will come back to us manyfold, believe me—I've been there. So remember, when it rains, think of Jesus; he is cleansing our souls. His tears are tears of sorrow, tears of joy, but more importantly, tears of hope that we can accept him into our hearts.

* * * *

RAIN OF TEARS

As I awakened
To the sound of falling rain,
I gazed out the window
And began to feel my shame.

For I realize that,
Although I walk in your light,

I still allow the darkness
To linger within your sight.

You have given all for me,
But I still let my heart sear.
Yet your love for me still shines through,
For the raindrops that fall are your tears.

The rain brings life.
Your tears show sorrow.
The rain can destroy.
But your tears show love and bring hope for tomorrow.

Why must I be torn
To love you but turn away?
To ask your help,
Yet hurt you everyday?

Please, Lord Jesus,
Teach me how to overcome.
Rip this evil from my heart,
And let it be done.

The rain falls
So gentle upon my face,
It makes me feel clean,
Your tears, which I taste

I can feel your love
As the rain pours down.
The sound of love,
Yes, it is the only sound.

The tears you cry.
For all your children
Shall wash away
Our wrong and our sin.

As the rain falls,
I am comforted and can now cope.
For I now shed tears of my own,
Tears of hope.

Chapter Seventeen
Man vs. God

ON A FINAL NOTE. As I grow closer to Jesus, I understand that although he is my friend, he is still the Lord. I need to learn to let go of the man-made rules of life and begin to follow the laws of God. I try to listen to the words of Jesus, and not only that, but to follow them.

Man complicates things; we take the simple and make it complicated and confusing. Man-made rules are overburdening; they bring destruction, but we can't see that, because we're right in the middle of it all.

When times get rough, I stop to think of what Jesus said, "Come unto me, all ye that labour and are heavy laden, and I will give you rest. Take my yoke upon you, and learn of me; for I am meek and lowly in heart and ye shall find rest unto your souls. For my yoke is easy and my burden light."

How can one read these words and not see the peace that he is offering to us? We can't see it, because, as I said before, we are right in the middle of all the chaos. We have lived our entire lives buried to our necks in man-made rules. What's worse is that we think this is normal.

Following Jesus can be tough. Here's another of his sayings. "Enter ye in at the strait gate: for wide is the gate, and broad is the way, that leadeth to destruction, and many there be which go in thereat: because strait is the gate, and narrow is the way, which leadeth unto life, and few there be that find it."

So I listen to his words, and I hear what he is saying to me.

I truly think that when we begin to follow Jesus, we do it with an honest heart. But sometimes, in our zeal to learn the word of God, or perhaps in our best efforts to spread the word of God, we cross the line between man and God.

Always remember, although we have found a friend, a true friend that loves us, he is much more than that. Man is nothing compared to God; man is a drop of water in the ocean of life, a mere speck of sand in the vast universe, man is nothing. With all of our technology today and with whatever advances we make in the future, we will still be nothing compared to God.

Man asks, "Who has the final word?"

I answer "God."

Jesus is our pathway to God. Again I listen to his words, "All power is given unto me in heaven and in earth. Go ye therefore, and teach all nations, baptizing them in the name of the Father, and of the Son, and of the Holy Ghost: Teaching them to observe all things whatsoever I have commanded you: and, lo, I am with you always, even unto the end of the world. Amen."

These are the words of our Lord Jesus Christ. I listen to them. I follow them. I love him, and I let him love me. He is there. He has always been there, and he will always be there. I call him my friend, but I try to never forget that he is my Lord as well. We go to him as a broken people, and he sheds his grace upon us.

An Invitation

I would like to invite all my readers to visit my web site. Here you will find more information on my journey with Christ. I'll be updating the site from time to time to reflect the status of projects that I'm working on, and I'll keep you up to date on how I'm doing.

I would also like to hear from you and get feedback on this book as well as on books to come. I would also like to know how you're progressing with your own journey. So please spend a few moments to visit and write.

May the love of Jesus embrace your heart and light your path.

Joseph R. Sgro

Web Site—http://home.earthlink.net/~joe.sgro
Email—joe.sgro@earthlink.net

Please Visit my new website at

www.thejourneywithchrist.com

About the Author

The author, Joseph R. Sgro—except for a two-year stint living in the city of Las Cruces, New Mexico—has been a lifelong resident of New Jersey. During his stay in Las Cruces, Joseph attended flight school and obtained his pilot's license.

After graduating from high school, he attended aeronautical school in Teterboro, NJ, where he received numerous class awards. Upon graduation he received both his airframe and power plant licenses. One can sense a strong attraction to aviation in Joe's background.

Working in the aerospace field at various levels, Joseph developed skills that would eventually assist him in starting his own business. With years of experience behind him, and having settled down in the rural countryside of New Jersey with his wife and daughter, Joe finally realized the dream of establishing a successful drafting firm.

When he began his journey with Christ, he developed a love for the scriptures. Seeing how much difference the love of Christ has made in his own life, Joe now wishes to help others find that love and to reconnect to the Lord.

Faith in Christ: The Journey Out of Loneliness, is Joseph's first book, however, it will not be his last. There is a calling to continue writing, and he will follow it.

978-0-595-42836-6
0-595-42836-3